Better Homes and Gardens®

Test Kitchen Favorites

Meredith Books
Des Moines, Iowa

Better Homes and Gardens® Books
An Imprint of Meredith® Books

Test Kitchen Favorites
Editor: Jan Miller
Project Editor and Writer: Winifred Moranville
Contributing Editor: Margaret Smith
Senior Associate Design Director: Mick Schnepf
Contributing Art Director: Brad Ruppert, Studio G
Copy Chief: Terri Fredrickson
Copy and Production Editor: Victoria Forlini
Editorial Operations Manager: Karen Schirm
Managers, Book Production: Pam Kvitne, Marjorie J. Schenkelberg, Rick von Holdt
Contributing Copy Editor: Jennifer Speer Ramundt
Contributing Proofreaders: Maria Duryée, Gretchen Kaufmann, Susan J. Kling
Photographers: Marty Baldwin, Jay Wilde
Food Stylists: Dianna Nolin, Charles Worthington
Indexer: Elizabeth T. Parson
Electronic Production Coordinator: Paula Forest
Editorial and Design Assistants: Karen McFadden, Mary Lee Gavin
Test Kitchen Director: Lynn Blanchard
Test Kitchen Product Supervisor: Marilyn Cornelius
Test Kitchen Home Economists: Juliana Hale; Laura Harms, R.D.; Jennifer Kalinowski, R.D. ; Maryellyn Krantz; Jill Moberly; Colleen Weeden; Lori Wilson

Meredith® Books
Editor in Chief: Linda Raglan Cunningham
Design Director: Matt Strelecki
Executive Editor, Food and Crafts: Jennifer Dorland Darling

Publisher: James D. Blume
Executive Director, Marketing: Jeffrey Myers
Executive Director, New Business Development: Todd M. Davis
Executive Director, Sales: Ken Zagor
Director, Operations: George A. Susral
Director, Production: Douglas M. Johnston
Business Director: Jim Leonard

Vice President and General Manager: Douglas J. Guendel

Better Homes and Gardens® Magazine
Editor in Chief: Karol DeWulf Nickell
Deputy Editor, Food and Entertaining: Nancy Hopkins

Meredith Publishing Group
President, Publishing Group: Stephen M. Lacy
Vice President-Publishing Director: Bob Mate

Meredith Corporation
Chairman and Chief Executive Officer: William T. Kerr

In Memoriam: E. T. Meredith III (1933-2003)

Reprinted from the 2003 version of *Better Homes and Gardens® Test Kitchen Favorites*

Our seal assures you that every recipe in *Test Kitchen Favorites* has been tested in the Better Homes and Gardens® Test Kitchen. This means that each recipe is practical and reliable, and meets our high standards of taste appeal. We guarantee your satisfaction with this book for as long as you own it.

All of us at Meredith® Books are dedicated to providing you with information and ideas to create delicious foods. We welcome your comments and suggestions. Write to us at: Better Homes and Gardens Books, Cookbook Editorial Department, 1716 Locust St., Des Moines, IA 50309-3023

If you would like to purchase any of our cooking, crafts, gardening, home improvement, or home decorating and design books, check wherever quality books are sold. Or visit us at: bhgbooks.com

Dear Friends,

In celebration of the diamond anniversary of the *Better Homes and Gardens* Test Kitchen, we proudly present 150 of our all-time favorite recipes, selected from our vast archives of recipes published since the kitchen was established in 1928.

In the last 40 years, we've published more than 60,000 recipes. So how did we choose 150 "greatest hits"? First, we asked the home economists currently on our staff. Some have been with us 10, 20, and even 30 years. No doubt about it— we've seen plenty of great recipes in our time! For this book, we collected our favorites, the ones we proudly share with family and friends.

We also asked former Test Kitchen home economists, women who joined our staff as early as the 1940s and who worked so hard to establish our good reputation. We hoped these veteran cooks could help us rediscover some terrific recipes, and we were right.

In fact, we found reams of old favorites and it was difficult to leave some out, but we think we've come up with the cream of the crop. It represents the full spectrum of great home cooking. Some recipes are all-out dazzlers we reserve for special celebrations; others include our favorites for everyday family meals. We couldn't resist including such heirloom recipes as Orange Bowknots and Apple Dumplings—time-honored *Better Homes and Gardens* classics that your grandmother may have made.

Of course, we couldn't leave out your favorites—the recipes readers most often request when they call in and tell us something like "My mother used to make your recipe for…Can you help me find it?"

Every one of our all-time favorites has recently gone through the same testing process that all of our new recipes do. (For a peek inside this rigorous process, take a look at pages 10 and 11.) We've ensured that each recipe has stood the test of time. And while we've updated the recipes for today's cooking techniques and tastes, we've made equally sure that each retains the personality and flavor of its era.

In addition to the recipes, we've filled the pages with vintage views of our Test Kitchen along with clippings from the magazines and books we helped produce throughout our 75 years. Plus, you'll get a look inside the Test Kitchen today and meet the home economists who proudly carry on the tradition of providing practical, reliable, and delicious recipes to America's home cooks.

We hope you enjoy this journey back as much as we did—and that our favorites become yours.

On behalf of your friends in the *Better Homes and Gardens* Test Kitchen, I wish you much joy in the kitchen and around your table.

Sincerely,

Lynn Blanchard

Lynn Blanchard
Test Kitchen Director

Favorites from the '80s......page 120

Let's do brunch, then check out Lemon Tarragon Chicken Fricassee, Coq au Vin Rosettes, Exquisite Almond Truffles, and other choice recipes from the gourmet-food-loving '80s.

Favorites from the '90s to Now........page 152

Come see our favorite ways to take advantage of the wondrous range of fresh, stylish ingredients available to cooks today.

Our Favorite Showstoppers ....page 186

We've always loved a party! Call on these dazzlers when it's time to pull out all the stops for entertaining.

A "Thoroughly Modern" Kitchen

The range in the first Testing-Tasting kitchen was considered to be a housewife's dream of perfection—a range with plenty of oven space, two baking ovens, a broiler, warming oven, and storage closet.

I t all started in 1922, when a magazine devoted to home and family called *Fruit, Garden and Home* was published. In 1924 the name was changed to *Better Homes and Gardens* to more accurately reflect the magazine's mission. A year later, the magazine's food editors created the "Cook's Round Table," giving us a column to help readers share their favorite recipes. At that time, food editor Genevieve Callahan tested the recipes in her own home kitchen.

In 1928, the first in-house test kitchen, located just across the hall from the *Better Homes and Gardens* editorial offices, was established. Called the "Testing-Tasting Kitchen," this facility had taken years of planning. As the editors told readers in the 1929 feature, *opposite*, "It was remodeled and rearranged dozens of times on paper before it took form in wood and plaster."

The staff was proud of the many step-saving devices in its "thoroly modern kitchen" (the reason for the variant spelling of "thoroughly," which often appears on our early food pages, has been lost to history). Advances in the new kitchen included cupboards built around the refrigerator and a worktable that also served as a dining surface. There were an enormous sink and gas stove; colored enamelware on the counters and ledges matched the woodwork and kitchen curtains.

Most important, the facility for testing and tasting recipes was "a modern workshop as near as possible in size and equipment to what you might find in a home." While it's now called the Test Kitchen and has been remodeled and updated many times during the past 75 years, that aspect has remained constant to this day: We use the same equipment as most home cooks to make sure every recipe can be duplicated exactly in your kitchen.

The Evolution of Recipe Writing

O ne of the earliest goals of the Test Kitchen was to nudge the American public into a new, more scientific era of cooking. This included a major overhaul in the way recipes were written. Before this revolution, a recipe for Currant Pie would have read something like this:

> **Add one cup of raspberries to three cups of ripe currants and bake in two crusts. Serve plain or with whipped cream.**

The writers of such a recipe would assume that—why, of course—any cook knows how to make a piecrust, how to prepare the fruit to use in the pie, how long to bake the pie, and at what temperature to bake the pie. And doesn't every cook just know she needs to add some sugar to sweeten the fruit, plus starch to thicken it?

Our experience convinced us otherwise, so the *Better Homes and Gardens* Test Kitchen came to the rescue of home cooks. The Test Kitchen championed a new style of recipe writing that called on level measurements (no more "little bit of this or little bit of that") and more precise, descriptive methods (no more "bake till done"). Cooks all over America looked to our pages for practical, reliable recipes that were informative and easy to follow. And 75 years later, they still do.

Views of interesting corners in the Better Homes and Gardens' new "testing-tasting" kitchen. These pictures were drawn from photographs. Below, a tasting nook at the west end of the kitchen is directly opposite the sink and work-table shown in the center. The little, modern table has a surprising capacity for cookbooks and toys, as well as for the many delicacies tested

Our New "Test-ing-Tasting" Kitchen

It Is Thoroly Modern in Equipment and Furnishings

JOSEPHINE WYLIE
Associate Editor, Director of the Home Department

*Drawings by
Louise C. Rumley*

Step-saving devices wherever possible delight good homemakers. In the picture below, we show the convenient cupboards built around the electric refrigerator, and a smart little stool which inverted becomes a stepladder by which the higher shelves may be reached. Gay enameled ware matches the woodwork and the curtains

A real home kitchen in every sense of the word is our new "testing-tasting" kitchen! This kitchen, located just across the hall from the Better Homes and Gardens' editorial offices, is the result of an idea to establish a modern workshop as near as possible in size and equipment to what you might find in a home. Years of thought and planning went into the making of it. It was remodeled and rearranged dozens of times on paper before it took form in wood and plaster and was finally equipped in the most convenient and modern manner. We are proud of it, because it is a beautiful kitchen, and because it makes possible an even greater service to our many readers

The home economists in our Test Kitchen today, from left: Juliana Hale, Lynn Blanchard, Lori Wilson, Jennifer Kalinowski, Marilyn Cornelius, Jill Moberly, Colleen Weeden, and Maryellyn Krantz.

Our Test Kitchen Today

It's been 75 years since the first home economist in the ***Better Homes and Gardens*** Testing-Tasting Kitchen tied on an apron; got out her measuring spoons; and tested, tasted, and perfected the first recipe. Since then more than 60,000 recipes have successfully passed the rigors of our testing to be printed in a myriad of ***Better Homes and Gardens*** publications. As you can imagine, the kitchen is a busy place filled with wonderful aromas and a constant hum of activity. Here's a glimpse inside:

Who are the Test Kitchen home economists? All are trained professionals with bachelor of science degrees in food science, food and nutrition, culinary arts, or dietetics. All enjoy working with food, of course, but more specifically, they have a passion for understanding the science that underlies the art of cooking—they love to get to the bottom of how recipes work (or why they don't). When not testing, tasting, and checking recipes, they work hard to keep up with the latest trends and information about food, kitchen gadgets and equipment, and nutrition.

Each home economist tests an average of five recipes daily—a workload that would be impossible to handle without the help of a dedicated support staff including a grocery shopper who fills orders on a daily basis. That's quite a job! In fact, the grocery bill easily exceeds $100,000 annually, which includes 6,000 cups of flour, 4,000 cups of sugar, 4,800 eggs, and 600 pounds of butter.

About 90 percent of the groceries are purchased from local supermarkets, and we only test with national brands. This means that when we call for an ingredient, cooks across the country will be able to find it. If a recipe needs a special ingredient that requires a trip to a specialty store or is new to the marketplace, that information is included with the recipe.

We also have three housekeepers who help set up for taste panels and keep the kitchens clean and ready to go. The Test Kitchen office assistant Barb Allen tracks the recipes that go through our kitchen (with more than 6,500 recipe tests completed each year, that's not an easy task). Most important, she fields dozens of reader calls weekly.

Our Test Kitchen includes eight separate kitchens set up much like any home kitchen—each has a conventional oven, microwave oven, dishwasher, sink, garbage disposal, refrigerator, range (gas and electric), food processor, and mixer. That's it—no industrial ovens, hard-to-find gadgets, or specialized appliances. We use the same equipment most home cooks use.

During the past 75 years, our Test Kitchen has seen cooking trends come and go, and its appliances have been updated and replaced many times. But its mission has remained constant: To make sure every recipe in ***Better Homes and Gardens*** publications is delicious and easy to duplicate in your home.

"We are here for one reason. We want to ensure that when readers prepare recipes at home, they will be pleased with the results." —Lynn Blanchard, Test Kitchen Director

Our "Red Plaid" Tradition

In 1930, just two years after our Testing-Tasting Kitchen staff first began perfecting recipes for the home cook, another icon in American cookery came along: *My Better Homes and Gardens Cook Book.*

"Never before has there been a cookbook like this," exclaimed a full-page ad introducing the book—and it was true. Cooks loved the revolutionary ring binding, which allowed the book to open flat on the countertop. It was the first of its kind. And those clever tab dividers? Ingenious! When closed, the book resembled a mini filing cabinet, combining the advantages of both a book and a recipe card file for a true all-in-one kitchen resource.

Of course, no cookbook, no matter how neatly it lies flat on the counter, would be a best seller without top-notch, trustworthy recipes. And that's just what cooks found inside the *New Cook Book.* The foreword to the 1933 edition promised "the cream of thousands of tested and tasted recipes approved by the *Better Homes and Gardens* Testing-Tasting Kitchen." Recipes

were also written in an updated style (see page 6) that gave cooks everything they needed to know to achieve success. Cooks all over America took to the book—it became a best seller in three months, and by 1938, 1 million copies had been sold.

It wasn't until the 1940s, however, that the book, now titled *Better Homes and Gardens New Cook Book,* took on its famous red plaid design—a concept born of a chance encounter with a bolt of fabric. One noon hour, *Better Homes and Gardens* food editor Myrna Johnston spotted red-and-white gingham cloth at a local department store. On impulse, she bought a yard. Back at work, she and a colleague wrapped the cloth around the *New Cook Book.*

Maybe it seemed a little like a warm, welcoming tablecloth or was reminiscent of a home cook's apron. Perhaps there was something about the straightforward pattern that seemed honest and true. Whatever the appeal, it stuck. Today, 34 million copies later, the red plaid cookbook—now in its 12th edition—is an enduring symbol for trustworthy, reliable recipes.

Our Test Kitchen Seal

In 1933, the contest now known as the Prize Tested Recipes contest was created to recognize recipes sent in from cooks across the country that met "standards of taste and family usefulness." After readers' recipes were tested, the winners were published with our recipes-endorsed seal, *left.*

By 1959, our Test Kitchen seal had taken on the same red plaid design that graced the cover of our famous cookbook. Through the years, the seal has been used to give our stamp of approval not only to recipes submitted to the Prize Tested Recipes contest, but also to any and all recipes that have been tested and approved in our Test Kitchen. Our current seal, *below,* carries the promise that every recipe is "practical and reliable, and meets our high standards of taste appeal."

Everyone in today's *Better Homes and Gardens* Test Kitchen is proud of our "red plaid" heritage. We know that generations of home cooks trust this as a symbol for practical, reliable recipes. And like the generations of Test Kitchen home economists before us, we take this trust to heart.

The Recipe Trail

Ever wonder where our recipes come from and how they get from idea to printed page? Here's a look at the process.

A Great Idea...

Our recipes spring from numerous sources; sometimes one of our editors or home economists encounters a great idea when traveling, dining out, or enjoying meals with family and friends. Ideas also are born when new products enter the marketplace. Indoor grills, bread machines, slow cookers—all have inspired us to create new recipes.

Others ideas come from readers like you. Readers submit recipes to *Better Homes and Gardens* magazine's monthly Prize Tested Recipes contest. Winners are carefully selected after recipes are tested in the Test Kitchen.

Also, our editors, sometimes working with a network of recipe developers, create recipes to include in a particular book or magazine story. At this point the editors are essentially "cooking on paper," writing down their ideas for later testing. They note ingredients they'd like to include and ideas for how those ingredients might be cooked or mixed together.

No matter where the recipe comes from, it follows the same process for approval. Once it's conceptualized, it's submitted to the Test Kitchen.

...but will it work?

When the recipe arrives in the Test Kitchen, it's assigned to a home economist and testing begins. Our home economists read through the recipes first, then order the groceries. As they don their aprons and roll up their sleeves, the home economists ask all sorts of questions. Is the recipe practical? Will the steps, as written, make sense to a home cook? Are there steps that can be simplified or revised? Do the baking time and temperature seem accurate? Does the recipe adhere to the Test Kitchen's strict food safety guidelines?

Through this process, the home economists have readers and cooks foremost in their thoughts, suggesting any adjustments that will make the recipes easier on the cook—as long as the changes don't compromise the recipe's overall flavor and appeal.

Occasionally through testing, they find the steps that look great on paper fail to work in reality. And, like any home cook, the home economists have their share of mishaps—sauces may curdle, casseroles boil over, and things stick to the pan. That's when they use their food science backgrounds to analyze what went wrong and offer suggestions for the next test.

And above all, how does it taste?

Throughout the day, almost every workday of the year, the Test Kitchen holds taste panels where editors evaluate their dishes. A panel opens with the "tester"—the home economist who made the recipe—explaining how the recipe was prepared. After tasting the dish, an open conversation follows. Home economists and editors talk about flavor, texture, appearance, doneness tests, pan sizes, temperatures—lots and lots of details. If a recipe doesn't meet our standards for success, the home economist offers solutions for resolving the problems. Together, the

panel works to fix the recipe—ingredients are altered, cooking temperatures are adjusted, pan sizes may be changed, and new methods are tried. The recipe is scheduled for another test. Although some recipes sail through the Test Kitchen after one test, most recipes that appear in *Better Homes and Gardens* publications are tested at least three times.

If the recipe is a success, it's given a "publish" rating and the Test Kitchen seal is attached. Before it leaves the Test Kitchen, it's read one more time by someone who has not tested the recipe. This ensures that the recipe is complete and an editor will have all the necessary information to write the story.

In short, we put in of lot of kitchen time so you don't have to. We refine and tweak each recipe until we're sure it is easily re-created in a home cook's kitchen. Then, we taste and evaluate it to make sure it's a recipe you'll be proud to share with family and friends. If it doesn't meet our high standards, it doesn't appear on our pages.

Taste Panel Guidelines
Express unbiased opinions
Make constructive comments
Appearance
Flavor/Appeal
Texture
Doneness
Practicality (cost, time, method)
Suitability for project
How should it be served? Garnished?
Photo possibility
Keep things moving!
Summarize/classify

Decision for Retests
Is retesting necessary?
Will changes made provide desired results?
Is more research needed? Who will do it?
Who will evaluate retest?

Evaluating Retests
Were changes beneficial?
Is recipe now of publishing quality?
Have all options been tried?
(pans, methods, ingredients)

ABOVE: Posted in each panel room, these guidelines remind panel members to evaluate each recipe completely and objectively.

LEFT: A taste panel in our Test Kitchen today, from left: Winifred Moranville, editor; Jan Miller, editor; Jennifer Kalinowski, home economist; Lori Wilson, home economist; and Lynn Blanchard, Test Kitchen Director.

favorites from the

30s

1930

1933

1941

Journey back to the days when families gathered around the radio for their Saturday night entertainment and family meals were equally wholesome and uncomplicated. Stars of these decades include our classic Hamburger Pie, the original Chicken à la King, and other recipes that have warmed homes and hearts for generations.

The '30s & '40s in our kitchen

1933: *Better Homes and Gardens* announced a plan of recipe endorsement—now known as the Prize Tested Recipes contest. Entries were tested in our Test Kitchen, and winners received $1 and a Certificate of Recipe Endorsement. The contest continues to this day—perhaps the longest-running recipe contest ever.

1933

1928

1928: Our first in-house facility for testing recipes was introduced. Before this time, household editor Genevieve Callahan tested recipes in her home.

Best Cake Recipes

1929

1929: *Best Cake Recipes*, a collection of recipes from the *Better Homes and Gardens* Cake Recipe Contest, was published. Nudging cooks into a new, more scientific area of cooking, our Testing-Tasting Kitchen home economists called on standardized measures and precise cooking instructions. Hence, claimed the book, "it is harder to fail with cakes nowadays than it is to succeed."

1939: Styles in decor and dress may have changed, but the question inferred from this 1939 photo endures. What's for dinner? The first edition of the *Better Homes and Gardens Cook Book* appeared in *1930*, and we've been helping cooks answer that question ever since.

1939

Food and Appliance Trends: Homemakers enjoyed a whole new world of food preservation and preparation as the mechanical refrigerator, along with Clarence Birdseye's frozen fruits and vegetables, debuted in the 1930s and became household standbys by the 1940s.

1938

1938: The 38th printing of the fifth edition of our cookbook promised as always "Every Recipe Tested in the Better Homes and Gardens Testing-Tasting Kitchen."

"Thanks to Better Homes & Gardens
. . . we know how to increase our food supplies!"

1943

1943: Victory Gardens—home gardens meant to help with war-rationing efforts—sprouted up all over the country, and *Better Homes and Gardens* magazine was filled with Test Kitchen-endorsed recipes for pickling, preserving, and canning, as well as advice on how to get the most mileage out of homegrown vegetables.

15

Pomegranate seeds are one of today's happening ingredients, but this gorgeous salad from 1939 proves cooks long ago tapped into their delightful crunch and jewel-like tones. With sparkling dashes of color and bold sparks of citrusy flavor, the salad is a great way to brighten a winter meal.

Citrus-Avocado Salad

4	medium oranges	
2	ruby red grapefruits	
4	small ripe avocados, peeled, seeded, and halved	

¼	cup pomegranate seeds	
8	leaves red leaf lettuce	
	Celery Seed Dressing	

1. Peel and section the oranges and grapefruits, working over a bowl to catch juices; set juices aside. Reserve 24 orange sections; dice the remaining sections.

2. Slash rounded end of each avocado three times, cutting about three-quarters of the way to the opposite end each time. Turn flat sides up and insert an orange section in each slash.

3. Brush avocados with reserved fruit juices. Heap the diced oranges and grapefruit sections into avocados. Garnish with pomegranate seeds. Serve on lettuce with Celery Seed Dressing. (Refrigerate any remaining dressing for another use.) Makes 8 servings.

Celery Seed Dressing: In a small mixing bowl, blender container, or food processor bowl combine ½ cup sugar, ⅓ cup lemon juice, 1 teaspoon celery seeds, 1 teaspoon dry mustard, 1 teaspoon paprika, and ½ teaspoon salt. With mixer, blender, or food processor running, slowly add ¾ cup salad oil in a thin, steady stream. (This should take 2 to 3 minutes.) Continue mixing, blending, or processing until dressing reaches desired consistency. Makes about 1¼ cups.

Wilted Spinach Salad

6 cups torn fresh spinach
1 cup sliced fresh mushrooms
¼ cup thinly sliced green onions (2)
    Dash black pepper (optional)
3 slices bacon

¼ cup vinegar
2 teaspoons sugar
½ teaspoon dry mustard
1 hard-cooked egg, chopped

1. In a large bowl combine the spinach, mushrooms, and green onions. If desired, sprinkle with pepper; set aside.

2. For dressing, in a 12-inch skillet cook bacon until crisp. Remove bacon; reserving 2 tablespoons drippings in skillet (add salad oil, if necessary). If desired, substitute 2 tablespoons salad oil for bacon drippings. Drain bacon on paper towels. Crumble bacon; set aside. Stir vinegar, sugar, and dry mustard into drippings. Bring to boiling; remove from heat. Add the spinach mixture. Toss mixture in skillet for 30 to 60 seconds or until spinach wilts.

3. Transfer mixture to a serving dish. Add crumbled bacon and chopped egg; toss to combine. Serve salad immediately. Makes 4 servings.

This midcentury classic

dates back to the days of elegant dining rooms, when tuxedoed waiters flambéd the dressing ingredients and tossed the salad tableside. Throughout the years, our Test Kitchen home economists have had a knack for adapting favorite restaurant specialties into recipes easily made by home cooks. Try this at your next intimate dinner party—it ranks as one of those "I've forgotten how good this is" recipes, and your guests will love being reminded.

Salad toss

Everyone needs a terrific recipe for a good-old potato soup, and this 1943 version, flavored with bacon, endures as one of our best ever. Serve with a ham or turkey sandwich for a comforting and immensely satisfying lunch or supper.

Potato-Onion Soup

6 slices bacon
5 cups sliced red potatoes
3 cups water
1 tablespoon instant chicken bouillon granules

3 medium onions, cut into very thin wedges (1½ cups)
2 cups milk
¼ teaspoon black pepper

1. In a large skillet cook the bacon over medium heat until bacon is crisp. Remove bacon, reserving 1 tablespoon drippings in skillet. Drain bacon on paper towels. Crumble bacon; set aside.

2. In a large saucepan combine the potatoes, water, and chicken bouillon granules. Bring to boiling; reduce heat. Simmer, covered, about 15 minutes or until potatoes are very tender. Do not drain potatoes.

3. Meanwhile, cook the onions in the reserved bacon drippings over medium-low heat for 8 to 10 minutes or until tender and golden brown. Remove from skillet; set aside. Mash potatoes slightly with a potato masher. Stir in the bacon, onions, milk, and pepper; heat through. If desired, season to taste with additional pepper. Makes 6 servings.

The Original
Chicken à la King

1 cup thinly sliced mushrooms
½ medium green sweet pepper, finely
    chopped
2 tablespoons butter
2 tablespoons all-purpose flour
½ teaspoon salt
2 cups half-and-half or light cream
2 tablespoons butter, softened
3 egg yolks

1 tablespoon lemon juice
1 teaspoon onion juice (optional)*
½ teaspoon paprika
3 cups chopped cooked chicken
2 tablespoons diced pimiento, drained
1 tablespoon sherry
16 hot toast points or 8 baked
    pastry shells

1. In a large skillet cook the mushrooms and sweet pepper in 2 tablespoons butter over medium heat until tender. Stir in the flour and salt. Add half-and-half all at once; cook and stir until thickened and bubbly.

2. Stir together the 2 tablespoons softened butter and egg yolks. Add the lemon juice, onion juice (if desired), and paprika. Stir about 1 cup of the half-and-half mixture into the egg mixture; return to the half-and-half mixture in the skillet. Cook and stir over medium heat until bubbly. Stir in chicken, pimiento, and sherry; heat through. Serve over toast points or pastry shells. Makes 8 servings.

*Note: Find onion juice in the spice section of large supermarkets.

Did you know that, in spite of its name, this dish has nothing to do with royalty? According to the 1937 issue of *Better Homes and Gardens* magazine, the dish was developed in the kitchen of the Brighton Beach Hotel, outside New York City, for the hotel's proprietor, E. Clarke King. This luscious recipe is, according to King's son, the authentic version named for his father. We feel there's never been a better recipe for the classic.

Somerset Sirloin

2	pounds beef sirloin steak, cut 1½ inches thick	1	pound fresh mushrooms (such as button or shiitake)
1	tablespoon olive oil	¼	teaspoon salt
¼	teaspoon salt	⅛	teaspoon black pepper
¼	teaspoon black pepper	½	cup half-and-half or light cream
2	tablespoons Worcestershire sauce		Fresh cracked black pepper
2	tablespoons butter		

1. Brush both sides of steak with oil. Sprinkle with ¼ teaspoon salt and the ¼ teaspoon pepper. Place steak in a shallow baking dish. Drizzle with Worcestershire sauce. Cover and marinate in the refrigerator for 2 hours.

2. Transfer the meat to the unheated rack of a broiler pan. Broil meat 4 to 5 inches from heat to desired doneness, turning once. (Allow 16 to 20 minutes for medium rare or 20 to 25 minutes for medium doneness.)

3. Meanwhile, in a large skillet melt the butter over medium heat. Add the mushrooms, ¼ teaspoon salt, and the ⅛ teaspoon pepper. Cook mushrooms for 5 to 6 minutes or just until tender, stirring occasionally. Stir in the half-and-half. Bring to boiling; reduce heat. Simmer, uncovered, for 8 to 10 minutes or until half-and-half is slightly thickened. Place the steak on a serving platter; spoon mushroom sauce over. Sprinkle with fresh cracked black pepper. Makes 6 to 8 servings.

With this recipe, J.F. Ruhnka of Los Angeles took second prize in a men's cooking contest in the 1930s. About cooking, he said, "I learned to cook in the Navy, and, boy, the dishes I can concoct. It won't be long until we men will be tempting the appetites of our women-folk with intriguing new dishes." More than 70 years later, his creamy take on steak and mushrooms continues to tempt men- and women-folk.

These Recipes From Men Are Prizewinners

JOSEPHINE WYLIE

THAT the man-person very often chooses the meal is a quite generally accepted fact. Men and women both admit that it is he who guides the cooking program by his likes and his dislikes, his suggestions and his approbation.

Say we turn for a moment to what we have a right to expect is a fairly common breakfast-table conversation:

"What do you want for dinner tonight?" asks the wife.

"Corn beef and cabbage," answers the husband. And corn beef and cabbage it is.

But that the man of the family actually cooks—that has been a moot question. After looking over the hundreds of recipes submitted in the Men's Cooking Contest, conducted by *Better Homes and Gardens*, we have proof positive that he not only can cook but that he excels at it. It may look like a grand gesture when he takes hold of the cooking spoon, but when he turns out a hash—yes, a hash, the most lowly of dishes—to taste as superb as did the San Gabriel Hash submitted by H. C. Moore, of Morgantown, West Virginia, then we shall have to admit that he is good. We honestly wanted to give the first prize to something with a grander-sounding name, but the rest of the judges outvoted us. J. F. Ruhnka, Los Angeles, California, came very close to being first-prize winner; his "Somerset Sirloin" took second prize. Captain Frank Steiner, Carlisle, Pennsylvania, won third prize with "Chicken a la Dixie."

We might explain that in order to judge fairly the merits of the various recipes which rated high in the opinion of the judges, the dishes were prepared in the *Better Homes and Gardens* Testing-tasting Kitchen, and a committee of men was invited in to judge the merits of each dish.

The prizewinning recipes follow:

San Gabriel Hash

6 potatoes	1 "clove" of garlic
1 can of corn beef	2 medium-size tomatoes,
3 green peppers	peeled, or the equivalent
3 onions (small)	in canned tomatoes
	1 cupful of water

Cut up all these ingredients in a chopping bowl, then chop quite finely. Put into a large iron skillet with the cupful of water and let cook until the

One thing the men's recipes showed us—a man may get a great deal of "kick" out of cooking

vegetables are tender, keeping covered all the while. Season highly, using plenty of paprika and stirring occasionally to keep from sticking. When the vegetables are done, the hash is turned into a greased loaf pan and put in the oven for 20 or 25 minutes to brown on top.

Mr. Moore's comment: "This, served with hot rolls and maybe sweet pickles, is a great meal. Just try it. I concocted San Gabriel Hash while in California several years ago. It has been a tremendous 'hit' whenever I've served it."

When father creates a steak masterpiece he has a right to feel proud—and he does

Somerset Sirloin

Sirloin steak, cut 1½ inches thick	Worcestershire sauce
Olive oil	1 pound of fresh mushrooms
Salt and pepper to season	2 tablespoonfuls of butter
½ cupful of thin cream	

Marinate the steak in the olive oil, seasoned to taste with salt, pepper, and Worcestershire sauce, for 2 hours. Sear the meat first on one side and then the other; then broil more slowly until done. Cook the mushrooms in the butter and season with salt and pepper. Stir often. When cooked add the cream. Place the steak on a platter and cover with the mushrooms. Serve at once!

Mr. Ruhnka's comment: "I learned to cook while in the Navy, and boy! the dishes I can concoct. It won't be long until we men will be tempting the appetites of our women-folk with intriguing new dishes."

Chicken a la Dixie

1 boiled chicken	1 pint of cream
2 truffles	Salt, pepper, and mace
1 small can of mushrooms, or equivalent in fresh mushrooms	Yolks of 2 eggs
	2 tablespoonfuls of sherry jell

Prepare by cutting boiled, well-seasoned chicken into dice, truffles into bits, and mushrooms in halves. Put all in saucepan with cream, salt, pepper, and a dash of mace, and cook 12 minutes. Mix and pour into the well-beaten yolks of 2 eggs. Stir until cooked, into which add 2 tablespoon-

Our first Swiss Steak recipe appeared in the late 1930s and was seasoned only with a little salt, pepper, onion, and mustard. Over the years, the ingredients have changed to include more flavorful items, such as tomatoes, celery, and carrot. With this version, you can choose the cooking method—range top or oven—that best fits your needs.

Swiss Steak

1 pound boneless beef round steak, cut ¾ inch thick	1 small onion, sliced and separated into rings
2 tablespoons all-purpose flour	½ cup sliced celery (1 stalk)
¼ teaspoon salt	½ cup sliced carrot (1 medium)
¼ teaspoon black pepper	2 cups hot cooked noodles or mashed potatoes
1 tablespoon cooking oil	
1 14½-ounce can diced tomatoes with basil, oregano, and garlic	

1. Trim fat from meat. Cut into 4 serving-size pieces. Combine the flour, salt, and pepper. Use the notched side of a meat mallet to pound the flour mixture into the meat.

2. In a large skillet brown meat on both sides in hot oil. Drain off fat. Add undrained tomatoes, onion, celery, and carrot. Bring to boiling; reduce heat. Simmer, covered, about 1¼ hours or until meat is tender. Skim off fat. Serve with hot cooked noodles or mashed potatoes. Makes 4 servings.

Oven directions: Prepare and brown meat in skillet as above. Transfer meat to a 2-quart square baking dish. In the same skillet combine undrained tomatoes, onion, celery, and carrot. Bring to boiling, scraping up any browned bits. Pour over meat. Cover and bake in a 350°F oven about 1 hour or until tender. Serve as above.

Irish-Italian Spaghetti

1 pound ground beef	½ teaspoon chili powder
1 medium onion, chopped (½ cup)	½ teaspoon bottled hot pepper sauce
1 10¾-ounce can cream of mushroom soup	¼ teaspoon black pepper Dash cayenne pepper
1 10¾-ounce can condensed tomato soup	1 pound dried spaghetti
	½ cup finely shredded Parmesan cheese

1. In a large saucepan cook the ground beef and onion until meat is brown. Drain off fat. Add the soups, chili powder, bottled hot pepper sauce, black pepper, and ground red pepper. Bring to boiling, stirring often; reduce heat. Simmer, covered, about 45 minutes, stirring often.

2. Meanwhile, cook pasta according to package directions. Serve sauce over hot cooked pasta. Sprinkle with cheese; pass additional sauce and cheese. Makes 4 servings.

It's true. Midcentury cooks used a lot of condensed soup in comfort food classics like this flavorful, simple pasta dish. It boasts not one, but two, types of condensed soup. We still get requests for this recipe 60-plus years after it was first published. It's easy, it's tasty, and people can't seem to get enough.

This is basically a shepherd's pie, though we wouldn't have used such a worldly name back when it first graced our pages in the 1940s. Wholesome, satisfying, and easy to prepare, it's a classic winter warmer, and just the sort of weeknight fare that has brought families together for meaningful, enjoyable meals for decades.

Hamburger Pie

Mashed Potatoes
1 pound ground beef
½ cup chopped onion
½ teaspoon salt
Dash black pepper
2 cups loose-pack frozen green beans, thawed

1 10¾-ounce can condensed tomato soup
½ cup shredded process American cheese (optional)

1. Prepare Mashed Potatoes; set aside. In a large skillet cook the ground beef and onion until meat is brown and onion is tender. Drain off fat. Add the salt and pepper. Stir in thawed beans and soup; pour into a greased 1½-quart baking dish.

2. Spoon Mashed Potatoes in mounds on bean mixture (or, if desired, pipe Mashed Potatoes using a pastry bag and a large star tip). If desired, sprinkle cheese on the potatoes. Bake, uncovered, in a 350°F oven for 25 to 30 minutes or until mixture is bubbly and potatoes are golden. Makes 4 to 6 servings.

Mashed Potatoes: Peel and quarter 1½ pounds baking potatoes. Place potatoes and ½ teaspoon salt in a medium saucepan. Add enough water to cover. Cook potatoes for 20 to 25 minutes or until tender; drain. Mash with a potato masher or beat with an electric mixer on low speed. Add 2 tablespoons butter; season to taste with salt and black pepper. Gradually beat in enough milk (2 to 4 tablespoons) to make mixture light and fluffy.

It's interesting—this recipe was originally published in the 1930s as a special-occasion dish to be served in a chafing dish (which was unabashedly dubbed "the beau catcher" by young ladies serving special recipes in them to their boyfriends). Today, however, the Test Kitchen taste panel thinks it would make a quick and tasty "oops—forgot about dinner" recipe. Chances are, you have most of the ingredients on hand—and you don't need a chafing dish.

Savory Ham and Eggs

8 hard-cooked eggs	$\frac{1}{8}$ teaspoon paprika
$\frac{1}{2}$ cup finely chopped fully cooked ham	$\frac{1}{4}$ teaspoon salt
$\frac{1}{4}$ cup butter or margarine, softened	Dash black pepper
1 tablespoon chopped onion	1 14-ounce can chicken broth
1 teaspoon snipped fresh parsley	1 cup milk
$\frac{1}{2}$ teaspoon Worcestershire sauce	1 cup shredded process American
$\frac{1}{4}$ teaspoon prepared mustard	cheese (4 ounces)
3 tablespoons butter	Hot cooked rice or toast points
$\frac{1}{2}$ cup all-purpose flour	

1. Halve the hard-cooked eggs lengthwise and remove yolks. Set whites aside. Place yolks in a bowl; mash with fork. Add ham, $\frac{1}{4}$ cup butter, onion, parsley, Worcestershire sauce, and mustard. Fill egg whites with yolk mixture; set aside.

2. In a large skillet melt the 3 tablespoons butter over medium heat. Stir in the flour, paprika, salt, and pepper. Add chicken broth and milk. Cook and stir until thickened and bubbly. Cook and stir 2 minutes more. Carefully place filled eggs in skillet. Sprinkle with cheese. Cook, covered, for 5 minutes more or until cheese is melted. Serve with hot cooked rice or toast points. Makes 5 to 6 servings.

Turnips au Gratin

2 pounds turnips, peeled and cubed (about 6 cups)

3 tablespoons butter or margarine

3 tablespoons all-purpose flour

¼ teaspoon salt

⅛ teaspoon black pepper

2 cups milk

½ cup shredded American cheese (2 ounces)

1½ cups soft bread crumbs (about 2 slices)

2 tablespoons butter or margarine, melted

1. In a large saucepan cook the cubed turnips in boiling water for 6 to 8 minutes or until nearly tender. Drain well in a colander. In same saucepan melt the 3 tablespoons butter. Stir in the flour, salt, and pepper. Add milk all at once. Cook and stir over medium heat until thickened and bubbly. Remove from heat; add the shredded cheese, stirring until melted. Stir in the cooked turnips. Transfer to a 2-quart square baking dish.

2. Combine bread crumbs and the 2 tablespoons melted butter. Sprinkle over the turnip mixture. Bake in a 375°F oven about 20 minutes or until crumbs are golden brown. Makes 6 to 8 servings.

The Cook's Round Table

contributor who submitted this recipe in 1932 boasted that with her recipe there was "less nip to the turnip." Back then, turnips and other root vegetables were one of the winter dependables that could be stored in the cellar until spring gardens thrived again. Turnips are now enjoying a revival in French-influenced cookery. This casserole makes a luscious and unexpected side dish for a dinner party or potluck buffet.

Oven meals—meals in which the main course, sides, and dessert were cooked at the same temperature in the oven—were popular during the 1940s because they helped with energy-saving war rationing efforts. This rich, yummy recipe is a great find from that era. Serve it with a simple roast or as part of a holiday buffet.

Scalloped Spinach

3 10-ounce packages frozen chopped spinach, thawed and well drained	¼ cup finely chopped onion
	¾ teaspoon salt
4 eggs, beaten	¼ teaspoon black pepper
¾ cup milk	1 cup soft bread crumbs
1 cup shredded processed American cheese (4 ounces)	1 tablespoon butter, melted

1. In a large bowl combine the spinach, eggs, milk, ¾ cup of the cheese, onion, salt, and pepper. Spoon into a greased 1½-quart straight-sided round baking dish (about 8-inch diameter). Bake in a 350°F oven for 50 minutes.

2. In a small bowl combine remaining cheese, crumbs, and butter; sprinkle around outer edge of spinach mixture. Bake 10 to 15 minutes more or until a knife inserted 1 inch from the center comes out clean. Let stand 10 minutes before serving. Makes 6 to 8 servings.

Spoon Bread Soufflé

3	egg yolks	1	tablespoon sugar
3	egg whites	1¼	teaspoons salt
4	cups milk		Dash black pepper
1	cup yellow cornmeal	1	tablespoon butter or margarine
¼	cup chopped onion		Butter (optional)
¼	cup chopped celery		Maple syrup (optional)

1. Allow the egg yolks and egg whites to stand at room temperature for 30 minutes. Slightly beat egg yolks.

2. In a large saucepan combine the milk, cornmeal, onion, celery, sugar, salt, and pepper. Cook and stir over medium-high heat about 10 minutes or until thickened and bubbly. Reduce heat to low; cook 2 minutes more, stirring frequently (watch carefully, as cornmeal mixture may bubble). Remove from heat. Gradually add 1 cup of the cornmeal mixture to beaten egg yolks; return to the cornmeal mixture in the saucepan.

3. In a large mixing bowl beat egg whites with an electric mixer on medium to high speed until stiff peaks form (tips stand straight). Fold egg whites into the hot mixture. Turn into a greased 2-quart casserole. Dot with 1 tablespoon butter. Bake in a 325°F oven for 1 hour or until a knife inserted near center comes out clean. Serve warm, with additional butter and maple syrup, if desired. Soufflé will settle as it stands. Makes 8 servings.

When your casserole runs the competition of the potluck table and disappears to the very last bite, you can count on it as an unqualified success.

Here's another recipe from the popular oven-meals trend of the 1940s. Today, as then, it makes a rich and intriguing side dish to serve in place of mashed potatoes. Also try the maple syrup option with sausages and toast as a breakfast dish.

This prizewinning recipe

from 1946 has kept up with our tastes so well that it has appeared in many of our publications since. A reader recently wrote, "When I saw the recipe, I cried in the bookstore! I won a baking contest with it in 1954—and bake them from my old margarine-stained cookbook at least once or twice a year." For that, and many reasons, this recipe is especially dear to our hearts.

Orange Bowknots

5¼	to 5¾ cups all-purpose flour		2	eggs
1	package active dry yeast		2	tablespoons finely shredded orange peel
1¼	cups milk			
½	cup butter, margarine, or shortening		¼	cup orange juice
⅓	cup granulated sugar			Orange Icing
1	teaspoon salt			

1. In a large mixing bowl combine 2 cups of the flour and the yeast; set aside. In a saucepan heat and stir the milk, butter, sugar, and salt just until warm (120°F to 130F°) and butter almost melts. Add to flour mixture along with eggs. Beat with an electric mixer on low to medium speed for 30 seconds, scraping bowl constantly. Beat on high speed for 3 minutes. Using a wooden spoon, stir in the shredded orange peel, orange juice, and as much of the remaining flour as you can.

2. Turn out dough onto a lightly floured surface. Knead in enough of the remaining flour to make a moderately soft dough that is smooth and elastic (3 to 5 minutes total). Shape dough into a ball. Place dough in a lightly greased bowl, turning once to grease surface of dough. Cover; let rise in a warm place until double in size (about 1 hour).

3. Punch down dough. Turn out onto a lightly floured surface. Divide in half. Cover and let rest for 10 minutes. Meanwhile, lightly grease two baking sheets; set aside.

4. Roll each half of dough to a 12×7-inch rectangle. Cut each rectangle into twelve 7-inch-long strips. Tie each strip into a loose knot. Place knots 2 inches apart on prepared baking sheets. Cover and let rise in a warm place until nearly double (about 30 minutes).

5. Bake in a 400°F oven for 12 minutes or until golden. Immediately remove from baking sheets. Cool on wire racks. Drizzle with Orange Icing. Makes 24 rolls.

Orange Icing: In a small bowl stir together 1 cup sifted powdered sugar, 1 teaspoon finely shredded orange peel, and enough orange juice (1 to 2 tablespoons) to make an icing of drizzling consistency.

*Try feather-light
Orange Bowknots—
you'll be voted
best cook in town!*

Better Homes and Gardens food editor Richard Swearinger rediscovered these delights as he looked through a 1925 issue. Now the cookies are his all-time favorite. "They're simple; they're great; they're everything a cookie should be," he says. We particularly love the way just three ingredients stack up to such a lovely, elegant cookie.

Hickory Nut Macaroons

4 egg whites	2 cups chopped hickory nuts, black
4 cups sifted powdered sugar	walnuts, or pecans, toasted

1. In a large mixing bowl beat the egg whites with an electric mixer on high speed until soft peaks form (tips curl). Gradually add the powdered sugar, about ¼ cup at a time, beating at medium speed just until well combined. Beat on high speed until stiff peaks form (tips stand straight). By hand, fold in the nuts. Drop mixture by rounded teaspoons 2 inches apart on a greased foil-lined cookie sheet.

2. Bake in 325°F oven about 15 minutes or until very lightly browned (cookies will puff and sides will split during baking). Transfer cookies to wire racks; cool. Makes 36 cookies.

To store: Place in layers separated by waxed paper in an airtight container; cover. Store at room temperature for up to 2 days or freeze for up to 3 months.

Cherry Winks

½ **cup sugar**	1 **cup all-purpose flour**
⅓ **cup shortening**	½ **cup chopped raisins**
½ **teaspoon baking powder**	½ **cup chopped walnuts**
¼ **teaspoon salt**	1 **teaspoon finely shredded lemon peel**
1 **egg**	2 **cups wheat flakes cereal, crushed**
1 **tablespoon milk**	18 **candied cherries, halved**
1 **teaspoon vanilla**	

1. In a large mixing bowl beat the sugar, shortening, baking powder, and salt with an electric mixer on medium to high speed for 30 seconds. Beat in the egg, milk, and vanilla until combined. Beat in as much of the flour as you can with the mixer. Stir in remaining flour with a wooden spoon. Stir in raisins, walnuts, and lemon peel.

2. Drop a teaspoonful of dough into crushed wheat flakes. Toss lightly to coat dough with flakes. Place cookies 2 inches apart on an ungreased cookie sheet. Top each cookie with a candied cherry half. Bake in a 400°F oven for 7 to 8 minutes or until bottoms are lightly browned. Transfer cookies to wire racks; cool. Makes 36 cookies.

To store: Place in layers separated by waxed paper in an airtight container; cover. Store at room temperature for up to 3 days or freeze for up to 3 months.

Cookies that have tiny dents filled with jellies and jams have been called by several names over the years—Thumbprints, Thimble Cookies, and Wee Tom Thumbs. In this playfully named 1945 recipe from our archives of prizewinning recipes, candied cherries stand in for the jelly.

With all the goodies we bake in our Test Kitchen, you'd think that bringing in cookies to share with the Test Kitchen staff at Christmas would be an exercise in overabundance. It never stopped Doris Eby, retired food editor, from sharing these family favorites with her colleagues every holiday season. Besides, there's always room for these spicy bite-size cookies, no matter how many other treats are around!

Pfeffernuesse

⅓	cup molasses	½	teaspoon baking soda
¼	cup butter	¼	teaspoon ground cardamom
2	cups all-purpose flour	¼	teaspoon ground allspice
¼	cup packed brown sugar	⅛	teaspoon black pepper
¾	teaspoon ground cinnamon	1	egg, beaten

1. In a small saucepan combine the molasses and butter. Cook and stir over low heat until butter melts. Remove saucepan from heat. Pour mixture into a large bowl and cool to room temperature.

2. In a medium bowl stir together the flour, brown sugar, cinnamon, baking soda, cardamom, allspice, and pepper. Set aside.

3. Stir egg into cooled molasses mixture. Gradually stir in flour mixture until combined; knead in the last of the flour mixture by hand, if necessary. Cover and chill about 1 hour or until dough is easy to handle.

4. Divide dough into 12 portions. On a lightly floured surface roll each portion into a 10-inch rope. Cut ropes into ½-inch pieces. Place pieces ½ inch apart in an ungreased shallow baking pan.

5. Bake in 350°F oven about 10 minutes or until edges are firm and bottoms are lightly browned. Transfer cookies to paper towels; cool. Makes 240 small cookies.

To store: Place in layers separated by waxed paper in an airtight container; cover. Store at room temperature for up to 3 days or freeze for up to 3 months.

Pfefferneuse, Hickory Nut Macaroons, page 32, and Cherry Winks, page 33

It's interesting how our recipe writing has changed over the years. When this recipe was first published in 1938, we instructed the cook to roll the dough "like a jelly roll," because back then, everyone knew exactly what a jelly roll was (and, most likely, how to roll one). While today's terminology has been updated , this cobbler-like dessert is still as wonderfully delicious as ever.

Blueberry Rolls

2 16½-ounce cans blueberries	½ teaspoon ground cinnamon
Rich Shortcake	¼ cup sugar
1 tablespoon butter or margarine,	2 tablespoons all-purpose flour
melted	2 teaspoons lemon juice
2 tablespoons sugar	Vanilla ice cream (optional)

1. Drain blueberries, reserving juice; set aside. Grease a 2-quart square baking dish; set aside. Prepare Rich Shortcake dough. On a lightly floured surface, roll dough into an 11×9-inch rectangle. Brush dough with melted butter. Combine the 2 tablespoons sugar with the cinnamon; sprinkle over dough. Sprinkle with 1 cup of the drained blueberries. Roll up into a spiral, starting from a short side. Seal seam. Slice roll into 9 equal pieces.

2. In a small saucepan combine the ¼ cup sugar and the flour. Add remaining blueberries and reserved juice. Cook and stir until thickened and bubbly. Remove from heat; stir in lemon juice. Pour blueberry mixture into prepared dish. Place rolls, cut sides down, on top of blueberry mixture. Bake in a 425°F oven for 20 minutes or until rolls are golden. If desired, serve warm with vanilla ice cream. Makes 9 servings.

Rich Shortcake: In a medium bowl combine 2 cups all-purpose flour, 4 teaspoons baking powder, 1 tablespoon sugar, and ½ teaspoon salt. With a pastry blender, cut in ⅓ cup shortening until mixture resembles coarse crumbs. Make a well in the center of mixture. Add ⅔ cup milk and 1 beaten egg all at once. Stir just until dough clings together. On a heavily floured surface, coat the dough lightly with flour. Knead the dough gently for 10 to 12 strokes.

Date-Nut Pudding

1 cup chopped pitted dates	½ cup light-color corn syrup
½ cup boiling water	1 teaspoon vanilla
1 tablespoon butter	1 cup chopped walnuts
1½ cups all-purpose flour	½ cup butter or margarine
1½ teaspoons baking powder	1 cup packed brown sugar
½ teaspoon salt	2 tablespoons light-color corn syrup
1 beaten egg	½ cup whipping cream
½ cup granulated sugar	

1. In a small bowl combine the dates, boiling water, and 1 tablespoon butter; set aside. In a medium bowl stir together the flour, baking powder, and salt; set aside.

2. In a medium bowl combine the egg, granulated sugar, the ½ cup corn syrup, and the vanilla; beat thoroughly. Stir in date mixture and flour mixture. Stir in the walnuts. Pour into a greased 11×7½×1½-inch baking pan.

3. Bake in a 350°F oven for 30 to 35 minutes or until a wooden toothpick inserted near center comes out clean; cool slightly.

4. Meanwhile, for the sauce, in a medium saucepan combine the ½ cup butter, the brown sugar, and the 2 tablespoons corn syrup. Cook and stir over medium heat until mixture comes to a full boil. Stir in the whipping cream. Return to a full boil. Remove from heat. Serve warm sauce with pudding. Makes 12 servings.

Although this pudding is truly more like a cake than a pudding, we kept the name because "pudding" is an old-fashioned word for dessert. And this 1945 treasure is a wonderfully old-fashioned dessert indeed! Hint: Refrigerate any leftover sauce. Reheat it another time to serve over ice cream.

Here it is—the first-place prizewinner of our first cake recipe contest, held in 1929, and chosen from more than 8,000 entries. In the foreword to the booklet of prizewinners, editors wrote, "We are quite convinced that most women would rather bake the perfect cake than be President of the United States." Whether or not that's true today, this absolutely elegant cake still reigns as a showstopper that would make any cook proud.

This delicious Pineapple-Meringue cake was awarded first prize in the Better Homes and Gardens cake recipe contest.

Pineapple Meringue Cake

¼ cup butter, softened	1 teaspoon vanilla
½ cup granulated sugar	½ teaspoon rum extract
2 egg yolks	½ cup granulated sugar
½ teaspoon vanilla	½ cup chopped pecans
1 cup all-purpose flour	1 cup whipping cream
1½ teaspoons baking powder	2 tablespoons powdered sugar
¼ teaspoon salt	1 teaspoon vanilla
½ cup milk	1 8-ounce can crushed pineapple,
2 egg whites	drained

1. In a large mixing bowl beat butter with an electric mixer on medium to high speed for 30 seconds. Add ½ cup granulated sugar and beat until well combined; add the egg yolks and the ½ teaspoon vanilla. Beat until light and fluffy. Stir together the flour, baking powder, and salt. Alternately add flour mixture and milk to creamed mixture. Pour into 2 greased and floured 8×1½-inch round cake pans.

2. Wash and dry beaters. In a medium mixing bowl beat the egg whites, the 1 teaspoon vanilla, and rum extract until soft peaks form (tips curl). Gradually add ½ cup granulated sugar. Beat until stiff peaks form (tips stand straight). Drop spoonfuls of egg white mixture onto unbaked batter in pans, then carefully spread to cover. Sprinkle pecans over egg white mixture. Press lightly into surface.

3. Bake in a 350°F oven for 25 to 30 minutes or until a wooden toothpick inserted in center comes out clean. Cool in pans for 10 minutes. Carefully remove from pans. Turn cake layers meringue side up; cool thoroughly on wire racks.

4. About 1 to 2 hours before serving, prepare filling. For filling, combine whipping cream, powdered sugar, and 1 teaspoon vanilla. Beat until soft peaks form. Fold in pineapple. Place one cake layer, meringue side up, on cake plate. Spread filling over top. Place second layer, meringue side up, on filling. Chill in the refrigerator for at least 1 hour but no more than 2 hours. Makes 10 servings.

1953

1954

1968

favorites from the

50s

The 1950s saw a return to peace and prosperity, as well as a baby boom in full swing. The overall exuberance of the times definitely made its way onto the family table with fun barbecues, lively salads, and plenty of family-friendly sweets. In the 1960s, recipes got a little more worldy and gourmet. Come savor our favorites!

60s

The '50s & '60s in our kitchen

1950s: The 1950s are often lovingly referred to as our "salad years." Although we had been developing recipes for main-dish salads since the '30s, the concept became a hit during this decade when businessmen found them to be a happy alternative to hearty fare. Lettuce salads also came of age during these years; in fact, Myrna Johnston, a *Better Homes and Gardens* food editor at the time, is often credited with coining the now-ubiquitous term "tossed salad."

1950s

1955

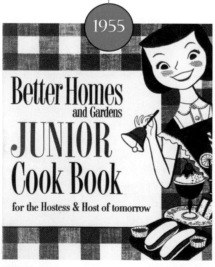

1955: The first edition of the *Better Homes and Gardens Junior Cook Book* debuted. Designed for the "hostess and host of tomorrow," it was filled with easy, kid-friendly recipes perfected in our Test Kitchen. Our love for bringing kids into the kitchen continues to this day—the *New Junior Cook Book* is now in its 6th edition.

1956

1956: "Dad's the chef. Sis and Brother kibitz, pitch in on tasks their size, and have the time of their lives. No kitchen chores for Mom." That's how *Better Homes and Gardens* editors described barbecuing in 1956. Developing hundreds of outdoor-cooking recipes throughout the 1950s, our Test Kitchen helped fire up America's enthusiasm for backyard grilling, and the popularity of this favorite pastime has never waned.

1960s: Words like tempura, Kiev, bourguignon, and cacciatore start to make their way onto the pages of our books and magazines, reflecting Americans' newfound love for foods from around the world. Since these times, our Test Kitchen has helped cooks bring international cuisine home using straightforward, easy-to-follow techniques and readily available ingredients.

1950s-1960s: "Jiffy cooking" became big news, as supermarkets brimmed with new convenience product wonders, including everything from packaged mixes and bottled dressings to canned meats, gravy, and more. Our Test Kitchen tested and perfected many a fast fix-up, proving again and again that—as our *New Cook Book* put it—"there's many a trick between the can opener and dinner that can make a hurry-up meal a really good meal."

1950s-1960s: Ensuring "recipe goodness," our Test Kitchen Seal signified that each recipe was "tested over and over till it rated superior—in both practicality and deliciousness."

1950s-1960s: Thanks to the rapid growth of supermarket chains along with improvements in air, freight, and rail shipping, shoppers were dazzled with exciting and exotic fruits and vegetables. Once-rare treats such as artichokes, shallots, tangelos, kumquats, Bing cherries, papayas, and mangoes popped up everywhere, and our Test Kitchen showed home cooks how to star them on their tables.

50s & 60s

Straight from the pages of the magazine published in the swinging '60s, this quick to whip up dip is quintessential good-time party fare. Serve it with mugs of Hot Buttered Rum, page 45, and rekindle all the footloose and fancy-free fun of the era.

Three-Cheese Spread with Almonds

1   8-ounce package cream cheese, softened
1   8-ounce carton dairy sour cream
1   cup shredded process Swiss cheese (4 ounces)
2   ounces crumbled blue cheese (½ cup)

1   tablespoon white wine Worcestershire sauce
1   teaspoon paprika
½   cup chopped almonds, toasted
    Crackers and/or party rye bread

1. In a medium mixing bowl beat together the cream cheese, sour cream, Swiss cheese, blue cheese, Worcestershire sauce, and paprika until light and fluffy. Cover; chill for up to 24 hours. Stir in nuts just before serving. Serve with crackers and/or bread. Makes 2½ cups.

Servantless service is no problem at the buffet meal.

The successful party begins with careful preplanning.

Hot Buttered Rum

2 quarts apple or pineapple juice
2 tablespoons brown sugar
3 inches stick cinnamon
1 teaspoon whole allspice
1 teaspoon whole cloves

¼ teaspoon salt
   Dash ground nutmeg
1 cup rum
¼ cup cold butter (no substitutes),
   sliced into 8 pats

1. In a large saucepan combine the juice, brown sugar, cinnamon, allspice, cloves, salt, and nutmeg. Bring to boiling; reduce heat. Simmer, covered, for 20 minutes. Stir in rum; return just to boiling. Remove from heat; pour through a strainer to remove whole spices. Place a pat of butter in each of 8 mugs. Pour the hot rum mixture into the mugs. Makes 8 servings.

When retesting this recipe,

our taste panel's comments included "I forgot how good this was!" "This is amazing! Why doesn't anyone make it anymore?" and "This is a great recipe to sip after you've settled up an argument with your significant other!"

Guests are always comfortable in a casual and friendly atmosphere.

To start a party moving, it helps to plan something that requires guest participation.

With the freshness of herbs, the tang of sour cream, and the irresistible bite of anchovy, a homemade Green Goddess Dressing is a wonderful thing. So how come few people make it anymore? We suspect one reason is bottled versions made everyone forget how great a freshly made version truly tastes. Try it, whether on this seafood salad or on a simple garden salad, and you'll agree that the classic is definitely due for a spirited revival.

Seafood Salad with Green Goddess Dressing

1 medium fennel bulb, cut into very thin wedges (1½ cups)	2 tablespoons sliced green onion
1 stalk celery, sliced (½ cup)	1 tablespoon vinegar
6 ounces fresh or frozen peeled, cooked shrimp	1 tablespoon snipped fresh basil or 1 teaspoon dried basil, crushed
6 ounces cooked lobster meat, cut into bite-size pieces	2 teaspoons anchovy paste or 1 large anchovy fillet, cut up
¾ cup packed fresh parsley sprigs	1 teaspoon snipped fresh tarragon or ¼ teaspoon dried tarragon, crushed
⅓ cup mayonnaise or salad dressing	
3 tablespoons dairy sour cream	1 clove garlic, halved
3 tablespoons plain low-fat yogurt	8 to 12 Bibb lettuce leaves

1. In a large salad bowl toss together the fennel, celery, shrimp, and lobster; set aside.

2. In a food processor bowl or blender container combine parsley, mayonnaise, sour cream, yogurt, green onion, vinegar, basil, anchovy paste, tarragon, and garlic. Cover and process or blend until nearly smooth.

3. Add ¼ cup of the dressing to shrimp mixture; toss gently to coat. Arrange lettuce leaves on 4 salad plates and top with seafood salad. Pass remaining salad dressing. Makes 4 servings.

Stuffed Flounder

2 pounds fresh or frozen flounder fillets (about 8 fillets)	**Dash** black pepper
¼ cup chopped onion	**3** tablespoons butter or margarine
¼ cup butter or margarine	**3** tablespoons all-purpose flour
1 4-ounce can whole mushrooms, drained and chopped	**1½** cups milk
1 6-ounce can crabmeat, drained and cartilage removed, and flaked	**⅓** cup dry white wine
½ cup coarse saltine cracker crumbs	**4** ounces process Swiss cheese, shredded or torn (1 cup)
2 tablespoons snipped fresh parsley	**¼** teaspoon paprika
¼ teaspoon salt	**Hot cooked brown rice, wild rice, or rice pilaf**

Here's one from the pages of the 1968 version of our famous "red plaid" cookbook. The flounder is filled with a crab-mushroom mixture, sauced with a hint of wine, and topped off with Swiss cheese. As the original recipe note claimed, it's "perfect for an elegant dinner." Hint: If your fillets are small, you can piece two together to form the roll.

1. Thaw fish, if frozen. Rinse fish; pat dry with paper towels. Set aside. In a medium skillet cook the onion in the ¼ cup butter until tender but not brown. Stir in the drained mushrooms, flaked crab, cracker crumbs, parsley, salt, and pepper. Spread crab mixture over flounder fillets. Roll up fillets into spirals and place, seam sides down, in 2-quart rectangular baking dish.

2. In a medium saucepan melt the 3 tablespoons butter. Stir in the flour and cook for 1 minute. Stir in milk and wine. Cook and stir until mixture is thickened and bubbly. Pour over fillets.

3. Bake in a 400°F oven for 15 minutes. Sprinkle with the cheese and paprika. Return to oven. Bake 5 minutes more or until fish flakes easily when tested with a fork. Serve with hot cooked rice. Makes 8 servings.

Cheesy Chicken-Corn Chowder

2 small skinless, boneless chicken breast halves (about 8 ounces total)	**1** cup frozen whole kernel corn
¼ cup chopped onion	**½** cup milk
¼ cup chopped celery	**½** cup shredded American cheese or cheddar cheese
1 cup water	**2** tablespoons chopped pimiento
1 10¾-ounce can condensed cream of chicken soup	

1. In a medium saucepan combine the chicken, onion, celery, and 1 cup water. Bring to boiling; reduce heat. Simmer, covered, for 15 to 20 minutes or until chicken is no longer pink. Remove chicken, reserving cooking liquid.

2. When cool enough to handle, chop chicken. Return chicken to mixture in saucepan. Stir in reserved cooking liquid, soup, corn, milk, cheese, and pimiento. Bring just to boiling, stirring until cheese melts. Makes 4 servings.

It might sound outdated to report "Men love this recipe!" but it's true: Men love this creamy and colorful, hearty and satisfying soup. Of course, our editors do too or it wouldn't be in this book. Though there's a can of soup in the mix, the easy add-ins make it taste fresh and homemade.

This recipe is famous around our Test Kitchen—and not just because it's a great version of the classic spaghetti with meat sauce. The story goes that one of our food editors, Sandra Mosley, received a marriage proposal after preparing this in 1970. Now that's some spaghetti!

Olive Spaghetti Sauce

1 pound ground beef	1 teaspoon sugar
½ pound ground veal	½ teaspoon chili powder
¼ pound bulk Italian sausage	1½ teaspoons Worcestershire sauce
1 cup water	3 bay leaves
1 teaspoon salt	2 4-ounce cans sliced mushrooms, drained (1 cup)
¼ teaspoon black pepper	½ cup sliced pimiento-stuffed green olives
1 28-ounce can tomatoes, cut up	20 ounces dried spaghetti, cooked and drained
1 12-ounce can tomato paste	Finely shredded Parmesan cheese (optional)
1½ cups dry red wine	
1 cup chopped onion	
¾ cup chopped green sweet pepper	
2 cloves garlic, minced	

1. In a large Dutch oven or kettle cook the beef, veal, and sausage until brown; drain off fat. Stir in the water, salt, black pepper, undrained tomatoes, tomato paste, wine, onion, sweet pepper, garlic, sugar, chili powder, Worcestershire sauce, and bay leaves. Bring to boiling; reduce heat. Simmer, uncovered, over low heat for 2 hours, stirring sauce occasionally.

2. Discard bay leaves. Add mushrooms and olives; simmer, covered, 30 minutes more. Serve over spaghetti. Pass Parmesan cheese, if desired. Makes 10 servings.

"I grew up with these!" notes one Test Kitchen home economist. Maybe you did too. Generations of kids learned to cook from the *Better Homes and Gardens Junior Cook Book*. This recipe comes from a 1950s edition of the classic—and we still get requests for it. Another testament? After taste panel, Test Kitchen pro Colleen Weeden took extras home for her kids. "They loved them," Colleen says. Fifty years later, they're still a hit. Parents, take the night off and let the older kids cook.

BAR-B-Q-Burgers

1	pound ground beef	1	tablespoon prepared mustard
⅔	cup chopped onion		Dash black pepper
1	10¾-ounce can condensed chicken gumbo soup	8	hamburger buns
¼	cup water		Sliced dill pickles (optional)
1	tablespoon catsup		Prepared yellow mustard (optional)

1. In a large skillet cook the ground beef and onion until beef is brown; drain off fat.

2. Stir in the soup, water, catsup, the 1 tablespoon mustard, and pepper. Bring to boiling; reduce heat. Gently simmer, covered, over low heat for 30 minutes, stirring occasionally. Spoon into 8 buns. Serve with dill pickles slices and additional mustard, if desired. Makes 8 servings.

Here's a page taken from the 1950s edition of the Better Homes and Gardens Junior Cook Book. *We simply omitted the unneeded fat in the updated version.*

BAR-B-Q-burgers

You'll need:

| 2 tablespoons fat | 1 pound ground beef | ⅔ cup chopped onion | ½ teaspoon salt | Dash pepper |

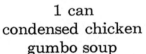

| ¼ cup water | 1 can condensed chicken gumbo soup | 1 tablespoon catsup | 1 tablespoon prepared mustard |

Take out:

Skillet
paring knife
measuring cups
   and spoons
can opener
wooden spoon
potholder

1 Cook meat and onion together in hot fat till meat is lightly browned. Stir frequently with wooden spoon

Cook about 30 minutes

2 Add other ingredients. Cover; simmer gently over *low* heat 30 minutes. Stir occasionally. Spoon into 8 buns

"Oh, so tender!"—that's what today's panel had to say about this 1950s grilled specialty. The original editors called it "the man's version of his wife's oven roast ... a specialty just as much as a bigwig cut of meat." What about the sauce? "Here's where you shine as an expert on herbs and spices," exclaimed the original note. "Flavor is the opposite of namby-pamby; consistency is nice and heavy. Dandy with roast pork or beef." We couldn't agree more!

Campfire-Style Pot Roast

19th Hole Sauce	6 small whole carrots, peeled
1 3½- to 4-pound boneless beef chuck	and halved
pot roast	1 medium green sweet pepper,
1 tablespoon cooking oil	cut in rings
Salt and black pepper	2 medium onions, quartered
Nonstick cooking spray	2 medium tomatoes, cut into wedges
2 stalks celery, bias-sliced into	
1-inch pieces	

1. Prepare 19th Hole Sauce. Meanwhile, trim fat from roast. In a Dutch oven brown pot roast on all sides in hot oil. Season lightly with salt and black pepper.

2. Meanwhile, fold two 5-foot lengths of heavy foil in half crosswise. Place one on top of the other, forming a cross shape. Lightly coat center of foil with cooking spray. Top with meat. Spread ¾ cup of 19th Hole Sauce on meat (cover and chill remaining sauce). Top with vegetables. Season lightly with additional salt and black pepper. Seal each piece of foil securely, allowing room for steam to build.

3. For a charcoal grill, arrange medium coals around edge of grill. Test for medium heat in the center of the grill. Place foil packet in center of grill. Cover and grill for 2½ hours or until meat is tender, adding additional charcoal as needed to maintain heat. (For a gas grill, preheat grill. Reduce heat to medium-low. Adjust for indirect cooking. Grill as above, except place packet in a roasting pan.) Place roasting pan on grill. Heat remaining sauce and pass with meat. Makes 6 servings.

19th Hole Sauce: In a medium saucepan stir together 2 tablespoons dried minced onion; 2 tablespoons brown sugar; 1 tablespoon whole mustard seeds, slightly crushed; 2 teaspoons paprika; 1 teaspoon dried oregano, crushed; 1 teaspoon chili powder; 1 teaspoon cracked black pepper; ½ teaspoon salt; ½ teaspoon ground cloves; 1 bay leaf; 1 cup catsup; ½ cup water; 2 tablespoons olive or cooking oil; 2 tablespoons red wine vinegar or cider vinegar; 2 tablespoons Worcestershire sauce; 1 clove garlic, minced; and 2 or 3 drops liquid smoke. Bring to boiling; reduce heat. Simmer, uncovered, for 20 to 25 minutes or until sauce reaches desired consistency, stirring occasionally. Remove bay leaf.

Oven Method: Trim fat from meat; brown as above. Drain off fat. Season meat with salt and black pepper. Spread ¾ cup of 19th Hole Sauce on meat in Dutch oven; add vegetables. Roast, covered, in a 350°F oven for 2½ hours. Transfer meat to a platter. Remove vegetables from cooking liquid with a slotted spoon. Heat remaining sauce; pass with roast.

Cherry-Almond Glazed Pork

1	3-pound boneless pork loin roast (single loin)	2	tablespoons light-color corn syrup
	Salt	¼	teaspoon ground cinnamon
	Black pepper	¼	teaspoon ground nutmeg
1	12-ounce jar cherry preserves	¼	teaspoon ground cloves
¼	cup red wine vinegar	¼	teaspoon salt
		¼	cup slivered almonds, toasted

1. Rub loin roast with a little salt and pepper. Place the meat on rack in a shallow roasting pan. Roast, uncovered, in a 325°F oven for 1½ to 1¾ hours or until thermometer registers 155°F.

2. Meanwhile, in a small saucepan combine the cherry preserves, red wine vinegar, corn syrup, cinnamon, nutmeg, cloves, and ¼ teaspoon salt. Cook and stir until mixture boils; reduce heat. Simmer, uncovered, for 3 to 5 minutes or until slightly thickened. Stir in the almonds. Keep the sauce warm.

3. To glaze roast, spoon some of the sauce over the roast the last 5 minutes of roasting. Cover meat with foil and let stand 15 minutes. The temperature of the meat after standing should be 160°F. Reheat remaining sauce; pass with meat. Makes 8 servings.

Sometime in the '60s, the Sunday roast got a lot more interesting, as this 1969 recipe—a favorite of longtime food editor Joyce Trollope—demonstrates. And if you've forgotten how nice gathering the family around a Sunday roast can be, call on this recipe to remind you. Hint: We reduced the roast size from the original recipe pictured, *left*, for a more family-friendly version. Belgian Creamed Potatoes, page 104, would make a dynamite serve-along.

Back in its day (1965, that is), this recipe might have been labeled an "easy oven meal." Today, we appreciate its fix-and-forget ease, and we also love the way it takes just five ingredients, not including water and pepper, to make such an intriguing, satisfying dish.

Spareribs Cantonese

4 pounds meaty pork spareribs or pork loin back ribs, cut into serving pieces

1 cup orange marmalade

¾ cup water

⅓ cup reduced-sodium soy sauce

2 cloves garlic, minced, or ½ teaspoon garlic powder

½ teaspoon ground ginger

Dash black pepper

Orange wedges (optional)

Green onion brushes (optional)

1. Place ribs meaty side down in a shallow roasting pan. Roast, uncovered, in a 450°F oven for 30 minutes. Remove from oven; carefully drain fat from ribs.

2. Turn ribs meaty side up. Reduce oven temperature to 350°F; continue roasting ribs, uncovered, for 1 hour. Carefully drain off fat. In a medium bowl combine the marmalade, water, soy sauce, garlic, ginger, and pepper; stir thoroughly. Pour over ribs.

3. Roast ribs, uncovered, for 30 minutes more or until tender, spooning sauce over ribs occasionally. If desired, serve ribs with orange wedges and garnish with green onion brushes. Makes 4 servings.

Take a big, creamy mound of mashed potatoes, shape it into a volcanic cone, add a little cheese and cream, and—oh boy!—you have just created an all-time kids' favorite. And whether you're a kid or just a kid at heart, you'll love this deliciously playful treatment of classic mashed potatoes.

Volcano Potatoes

1½ pounds baking potatoes (4 to 5 medium)	⅛ teaspoon black pepper
1 to 3 tablespoons milk	½ cup whipping cream
½ teaspoon salt	½ cup shredded sharp or regular American cheese (2 ounces)

1. Peel and quarter potatoes. In a saucepan cook potatoes, covered, in a small amount of boiling water for 20 to 25 minutes or until tender; drain. Mash with potato masher or beat with electric mixer on low speed. Gradually beat in enough of the milk to make light and fluffy. Stir in salt and pepper. Grease a 9-inch pie plate. Mound potatoes in pie plate, forming into a volcano shape about 3 inches tall and 5 inches across at the base, leaving a 1-inch space between potato mixture and edge of pie plate. Make a deep hole or crater in the center of the mound.

2. In a small bowl whip the cream until soft peaks form; fold in cheese. Spoon cream mixture into the hole, allowing the excess to flow down the sides. Bake, uncovered, in a 350°F oven about 20 minutes or until golden and bubbly. Makes 5 servings.

Cheddar Squash Bake

2 egg whites
6 cups thinly sliced zucchini (about ⅛-inch slices)
2 egg yolks, slightly beaten
1 8-ounce carton dairy sour cream
2 tablespoons all-purpose flour
¼ teaspoon salt

1½ cups shredded sharp cheddar cheese (6 ounces)
6 slices bacon, crisp-cooked, drained, and crumbled
1 tablespoon butter or margarine
⅓ cup fine dry bread crumbs

1. Allow egg whites to stand at room temperature for 30 minutes. In a large saucepan cook zucchini, covered, in a small amount of boiling salted water for 2 to 3 minutes or until crisp-tender; drain.

2. In a medium mixing bowl beat egg whites with an electric mixer on medium to high speed until stiff peaks form (tips stand straight).

3. In a large mixing bowl combine the egg yolks, sour cream, and flour; fold in egg whites. Place half the squash in a 2-quart rectangular baking dish; sprinkle with ⅛ teaspoon of the salt. Top with half the egg mixture, half the cheese, and all the bacon. Repeat layers of squash, the remaining ⅛ teaspoon salt, egg mixture, and cheese. In a small saucepan melt butter, stir in crumbs, and sprinkle over cheese layer. Bake, uncovered, in a 350°F oven for 20 to 25 minutes or until crumbs are golden and a knife inserted near center comes out clean. Let stand 10 minutes before serving. Makes 8 to 10 servings.

We've seen a lot of zucchini recipes over the years. Let's face it, during summer everyone's trying to figure out what to do with it! Here the squash is layered with cheese, bacon, and a rich egg mixture for one of our most elegant and interesting ways to serve this bountiful summertime veggie.

Cheese and corn in a creamy, custardlike base—we have to admit that we love it when something so simple turns out to be such a treat. Serve this alongside a baked holiday ham. Or take it to a potluck and watch it disappear fast.

Swiss Corn Bake

4 cups fresh corn kernels or two 10-ounce packages frozen whole kernel corn	Dash black pepper
2 beaten eggs	¾ cup shredded process Swiss or Gruyère cheese (3 ounces)
2 5-ounce cans evaporated milk (1⅓ cups)	¾ cup soft bread crumbs (1 slice)
2 tablespoons finely chopped onion	1 tablespoon butter or margarine, melted
¼ teaspoon salt	¼ cup shredded process Swiss or Gruyère cheese (1 ounce)

1. Grease a 9-inch pie plate or an 8-inch quiche dish; set aside. In a medium saucepan cook fresh corn, covered, in a small amount of boiling lightly salted water for 4 minutes. (Or cook frozen corn according to package directions.) Drain well.

2. In a medium bowl combine the corn, eggs, evaporated milk, onion, salt, and pepper. Stir in the ¾ cup cheese. Transfer corn mixture to prepared pie plate or quiche dish.

3. In a small bowl combine bread crumbs and melted butter. Stir in the ¼ cup cheese. Sprinkle over corn mixture. Bake, uncovered, in a 350°F oven for 25 to 35 minutes or until a knife inserted near the center comes out clean. Let stand for 5 to 10 minutes before serving. Makes 6 servings.

Potluck Potato Salad

6	medium potatoes (about 2 pounds)	3	hard-cooked eggs, coarsely chopped
¼	cup vinaigrette salad dressing, such as Caesar Parmesan, roasted garlic, dried tomato, or white wine vinaigrette*	½	teaspoon salt
		1	teaspoon celery seeds (optional)
		½	cup mayonnaise
			Paprika
1	cup chopped celery	1	hard-cooked egg, sliced
¼	cup chopped onion		Fresh parsley sprig (optional)

1. Scrub potatoes. In a medium saucepan place potatoes in enough water to cover. Bring to boiling; reduce heat. Simmer, covered, for 20 to 25 minutes or just until tender. Drain well; cool slightly. Peel and cube potatoes.

2. Pour the dressing over warm potatoes; cover and chill for 2 hours. Add the celery, onion, chopped eggs, salt, and, if desired, celery seeds. Add mayonnaise and mix carefully. Cover and chill for 4 to 24 hours. Before serving, sprinkle with paprika and top with sliced egg and parsley sprig, if desired. Makes 8 servings.

***Note:** Choose your favorite variety of salad dressing—just about any clear vinaigrette dressing will work.

Jean Brekke, now retired, started her first stint in the Test Kitchen in 1946. Since that time she's seen a lot of potato salads, and she stands by this one! Our taste panel loved the way the potatoes absorb the flavor and moisture of the vinaigrette dressing.

Two-Tone Bread

5	to 5½ cups all-purpose flour	⅓	cup shortening
2	packages active dry yeast	1	tablespoon salt
3	cups milk	3	tablespoons full-flavored molasses
⅓	cup sugar	2½	cups whole wheat flour

If you love to bake bread, add this recipe to your repertoire. The dark swirl not only adds loveliness to the loaf, but also a little molasses sweetness. Hint: The recipe makes two loaves. Enjoy one today and freeze one for the future. Or give the extra loaf as a gift—the recipient will be very grateful.

1. In a large mixing bowl combine 3¼ cups of the all-purpose flour and the yeast; set aside. In a medium saucepan heat and stir milk, sugar, shortening, and salt just until warm (120°F to 130°F) and shortening almost melts. Add milk mixture to flour mixture. Beat with an electric mixer on low to medium speed for 30 seconds, scraping sides of bowl constantly. Beat on high speed for 3 minutes. Remove 2½ cups of batter.

2. To the 2½ cups of batter, use a wooden spoon to stir in as much of the remaining all-purpose flour as you can. Turn dough out onto a lightly floured surface. Knead in enough of the remaining all-purpose flour to make a moderately stiff dough that is smooth and elastic (6 to 8 minutes). Shape dough into ball. Place in a lightly greased bowl, turning once to grease surface of the dough. Cover; set aside.

3. To remaining batter, use a wooden spoon to stir in molasses, whole wheat flour, and as much of the remaining all-purpose flour as you can. Turn dough out onto a lightly floured surface. Knead in enough of the remaining all-purpose flour to make a moderately stiff dough that is smooth and elastic (6 to 8 minutes). Shape dough into a ball. Place in another lightly greased bowl, turning once to grease surface of dough; cover.

4. Let both dough portions rise in a warm place until double in size (1 to 1¼ hours). Punch doughs down; divide each dough portion in half. Cover; let rest 10 minutes. Meanwhile, lightly grease two 9×5×3-inch loaf pans. On a lightly floured surface roll out half the light dough and half the dark dough, each to a 12×8-inch rectangle. Place dark dough on top of the light dough. Beginning from a short side, roll up tightly and shape into a loaf. Seal seams with your fingertips. Repeat with remaining doughs to make second loaf. Place in prepared loaf pans. Cover and let rise in a warm place until nearly double in size (45 to 60 minutes). Bake in a 375°F oven for 30 to 35 minutes or until bread sounds hollow when lightly tapped. (If necessary, cover loosely with foil the last 10 minutes to prevent overbrowning.) Immediately remove loaves from pans. Cool on wire racks. Makes 2 loaves (32 servings).

Freezing Bread: After the loaves have cooled completely, seal in a plastic freezer bag and freeze for up to 3 months. Thaw in package 1 hour or reheat in foil in a 300°F oven about 20 minutes.

If it's been a while since you've enjoyed a good, old-fashioned dinner roll, revisit the pleasure with these light, golden-brown buns—a prizewinning recipe from 1968. This makes a large batch, so freeze extras in freezer bags for up to 3 months.

Cornmeal Buns

6 to 6½ cups all-purpose flour	½ cup butter
1 package active dry yeast	1 teaspoon salt
2¼ cups milk	2 eggs
½ cup sugar	1½ cups cornmeal

1. In a large mixing bowl combine 3 cups of the flour and the yeast. In a saucepan heat milk, sugar, butter, and salt just until warm (115°F to 120°F), stirring constantly to melt butter. Add milk mixture to flour mixture in mixing bowl; add eggs. Beat with an electric mixer on low speed for 30 seconds, scraping bowl constantly. Beat on high speed for 3 minutes. Beat in cornmeal at low speed. Using a wooden spoon, stir in as much remaining flour as you can.

2. Turn dough out onto a lightly floured surface. Knead in enough remaining flour to make a moderately stiff dough that is smooth and elastic (6 to 8 minutes total). Shape dough into a ball. Place in a greased bowl; turn once. Cover; let rise in a warm place until doubled in size (1 to 1¼ hours). Grease thirty-six 2½-inch muffin cups.

3. Punch down dough. Turn dough out onto a lightly floured surface. Shape into 72 balls. Place 2 balls in each prepared muffin cup. Cover; let rise until nearly double (50 to 60 minutes).

4. Bake in a 375°F oven for 12 to 15 minutes or until rolls are golden brown. Immediately remove from cups to wire racks. Serve warm or cool. Makes 36 buns.

If you don't have 36 muffin cups: Place shaped dough balls on a waxed paper-lined baking sheet; cover with plastic wrap and chill while the first batch rises and bakes. After removing the baked rolls from muffin cups, wash pan, grease, and refill with chilled dough. Cover, let rise, and bake as above.

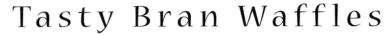

Tasty Bran Waffles

2	egg whites	2	egg yolks, beaten
1	cup all-purpose flour	1	cup whole bran cereal
¼	cup sugar	6	tablespoons butter or margarine,
1	teaspoon baking powder		melted
½	teaspoon baking soda		Whipped butter
¼	teaspoon salt		Syrup
1	cup buttermilk or sour milk*		

1. Allow egg whites to stand at room temperature for 30 minutes. In a mixing bowl stir together the flour, sugar, baking powder, baking soda, and salt; set aside.

2. In a large mixing bowl beat egg whites with an electric mixer on medium to high speed until stiff peaks form (tips stand straight).

3. Stir buttermilk and beaten egg yolks into flour mixture. Fold in bran cereal, melted butter, and stiff-beaten egg whites. Bake in a preheated waffle baker according to manufacturer's directions. Serve with whipped butter and syrup. Makes 8 (4-inch) waffles.

*Note: If you don't have buttermilk on hand, to make 1 cup of sour milk, place 1 tablespoon lemon juice or vinegar in a glass measuring cup. Add enough milk to make 1 cup total liquid; stir. Let stand 5 minutes before using.

Pancakes: To make pancakes from the batter, thin batter with additional milk, if desired. Bake on lightly greased griddle, using about ¼ cup batter for each pancake. Makes about 12 pancakes.

These rich, golden waffles won accolades all around at our taste panel, and everyone agreed wholeheartedly with the original note published alongside the recipe in 1966: "Whole bran cereal adds a nutty flavor to these waffles. Delicious for breakfast or Sunday supper!"

If you've never tried a chiffon cake, you must try this one! Richer than angel food cake yet just as airy and light, it practically shouts "Happy Birthday!" A note of nostalgia: Retired Test Kitchen pro Jean Brekke still remembers the day she made this cake in 1956 for food editor Myrna Johnston, who took it on the train to Chicago for a photo shoot. The editors then must have thought the cake was pretty special—and we do too.

Pineapple Chiffon Cake

5 egg yolks	½ cup cooking oil
8 egg whites (1 cup)	¾ cup unsweetened pineapple juice
2¼ cups sifted cake flour	½ teaspoon cream of tartar
1½ cups sugar	Pineapple-Buttercream Icing
3 teaspoons baking powder	Pineapple Daisies (optional)
1 teaspoon salt	

1. Allow egg whites and yolks to stand at room temperature for 30 minutes. Meanwhile, in a large mixing bowl combine the flour, sugar, baking powder, and salt. Make a well in the center of the flour mixture. Add oil, egg yolks, and pineapple juice in that order. Beat with an electric mixer on low speed until combined. Beat on high speed for 5 minutes more or until batter is satin smooth.

2. Thoroughly wash the beaters. In a very large mixing bowl beat egg whites and cream of tartar with an electric mixer on medium speed until stiff peaks form (tips stand straight). Pour batter in a thin stream over beaten egg whites; fold in gently. Pour into an ungreased 10-inch tube pan. Set pan on a baking sheet or pizza pan.

3. Bake in a 325°F oven for 60 to 70 minutes or until top springs back when lightly touched. Immediately invert cake (in the pan); cool thoroughly. Loosen sides of cake from pan; remove cake.

4. Frost cooled cake with Pineapple-Buttercream Icing. If desired, decorate with Pineapple Daisies. Makes 12 servings.

Pineapple-Buttercream Icing: In a large mixing bowl beat ½ cup softened butter with an electric mixer on medium speed for 30 seconds. Gradually add 2 cups sifted powdered sugar, beating well. Stir in 6 tablespoons well-drained crushed pineapple and 2 tablespoons pineapple juice. Beat thoroughly. Gradually beat in 2½ to 2¾ cups sifted powdered sugar until of spreading consistency. Spread on top and sides of cake.

Pineapple Daisies: Cut pineapple slices into thin wedges for daisy petals and use a maraschino or candied red cherry for flower centers and fresh mint for leaves.

Quick cake mix fix-ups never go out of style, and here's a favorite from our files. We found that a cake mix with pudding in it made a more moist cake than the mix without the pudding, though you can use either. And if you don't have time to make a homemade frosting, simply stirring a little peanut butter into the canned chocolate frosting, as directed, results in an almost-homemade-tasting solution.

Peanut Butter Crunch Cake

1 package 2-layer-size yellow cake mix	¼ cup chunky peanut butter
½ cup chunky peanut butter	1 16-ounce can chocolate frosting or
3 eggs	1 recipe Nutty Chocolate Frosting
1⅔ cups milk	

1. In a large mixing bowl combine the dry cake mix, the ½ cup chunky peanut butter, the eggs, and milk. Beat with an electric mixer on low speed until combined, scraping sides of bowl; beat for 2 minutes at medium speed. Spread batter into a greased 13×9×2-inch baking pan.

2. Bake in a 350°F oven for 30 to 35 minutes or until a wooden toothpick inserted near center comes out clean. Cool cake in pan on a wire rack.

3. Beat together the ¼ cup chunky peanut butter and the canned chocolate frosting, or use Nutty Chocolate Frosting to frost the cake. Makes 16 servings.

Nutty Chocolate Frosting: In a large mixing bowl combine 4¾ cups sifted powdered sugar, ½ cup unsweetened cocoa powder, and ¼ teaspoon salt. Add ⅓ cup boiling water, ⅓ cup softened butter or margarine, ¼ cup chunky peanut butter, and 1 teaspoon vanilla. Beat with an electric mixer until well combined. Makes about 2½ cups.

To cut your cake layer like this, choose a sharp knife with a thin blade. First, cut a circle about 2 inches from the edge of the cake. If the frosting is soft, dip the knife in hot water before you begin to cut the cake.

Now cut the cake as shown. From each slice you get 2 servings. Do not press down—hold handle of knife up and slice by pulling it toward you. You may get into family arguments over who gets outside pieces.

Our Best-Ever Chocolate Cake

¾ **cup butter, softened**	2 **cups sugar**
3 **eggs**	2 **teaspoons vanilla**
2 **cups all-purpose flour**	1½ **cups milk**
¾ **cup unsweetened cocoa powder**	**Chocolate-Sour Cream Frosting**
1 **teaspoon baking soda**	2 **cups chopped walnuts (optional)**
¾ **teaspoon baking powder**	**Chocolate-dipped walnuts, page 194**
½ **teaspoon salt**	**(optional)**

1. Allow butter and eggs to stand at room temperature for 30 minutes. Meanwhile, lightly grease bottoms of two 8×8×2-inch square or 9×1½-inch round cake pans. Line bottom of pans with waxed paper. Grease and lightly flour waxed paper and sides of pans. Or grease one 13×9×2-inch baking pan. Set pan(s) aside.

2. In a mixing bowl stir together the flour, cocoa powder, baking soda, baking powder, and salt; set aside.

3. In a large mixing bowl beat butter with an electric mixer on medium to high speed for 30 seconds. Gradually add sugar, about ¼ cup at a time, beating on medium speed until well combined (3 to 4 minutes). Scrape sides of bowl; continue beating on medium speed for 2 minutes. Add eggs, one at a time, beating after each addition (about 1 minute total). Beat in vanilla.

4. Alternately add flour mixture and milk to beaten mixture, beating on low speed just until combined after each addition. Beat on medium to high speed for 20 seconds more. Spread batter evenly into the prepared pan(s).

5. Bake in a 350°F oven for 35 to 40 minutes for 8-inch pans and the 13×9×2-inch pan, 30 to 35 minutes for 9-inch pans, or until a wooden toothpick inserted in the center comes out clean. Cool cake layers in pans for 10 minutes. Remove from pans. Peel off waxed paper. Cool thoroughly on wire racks. Or place 13×9×2-inch cake in pan on a wire rack; cool thoroughly. Frost with desired frosting. If desired, press chopped walnuts onto frosted sides of cake and top with Chocolate-dipped walnuts. Makes 12 to 16 servings.

Chocolate-Sour Cream Frosting: In a large saucepan melt one 12-ounce package (2 cups) semisweet chocolate pieces and ½ cup butter over low heat, stirring frequently. Cool for 5 minutes. Stir in one 8-ounce carton dairy sour cream. Gradually add 4½ cups sifted powdered sugar (about 1 pound), beating with an electric mixer until smooth. This frosts tops and sides of two or three 8- or 9-inch cake layers. (Halve the recipe to frost the top of a 13×9×2-inch cake.) Cover and store frosted cake in the refrigerator.

This recipe, while definitely rooted in the midcentury classic pictured on the 1952 cover, *below*, has been perfected over the years. We think you'll agree that this version is the moistest, richest, "chocolateiest" cake ever. And, of the many ways to frost it, we vote for our classic Chocolate-Sour Cream Frosting—though you can certainly use your own family favorite.

This pie, with its combination of rich chocolate sauce, refreshing peppermint ice cream, and airy meringue, impressed everyone when it first appeared in 1968—and it continues to dazzle to this day. Hint: If making a meringue sounds too fussy for you, replace the meringue topping with sweetened whipped cream.

A quick reputation as a good cook: Make a luscious pie!

Fudge Ribbon Pie

1	cup sugar	2	pints (4 cups) peppermint ice cream
1	5-ounce can evaporated milk ($\frac{2}{3}$ cup)	1	9-inch baked pastry shell, cooled
2	tablespoons butter or margarine	$\frac{3}{4}$	cup sugar
2	ounces unsweetened chocolate, cut up	$\frac{1}{2}$	cup boiling water
1	teaspoon vanilla	$\frac{1}{4}$	cup meringue powder
		$\frac{1}{4}$	cup crushed peppermint-stick candy

1. For fudge sauce, in a small saucepan combine the 1 cup sugar, the evaporated milk, butter, and chocolate. Cook and stir over medium heat until bubbly. Reduce heat and boil gently for 4 to 5 minutes, stirring occasionally, until mixture is thickened and reduced to 1½ cups. Remove from heat; stir in vanilla. If necessary, beat until smooth with wire whisk or rotary beater. Set aside to cool completely.

2. In a chilled bowl stir 1 pint of the ice cream until softened. Spread into cooled pastry shell. Cover with half of the cooled fudge sauce. Freeze until nearly firm. Repeat with remaining ice cream and fudge sauce. Return pie to the freezer while preparing meringue.

3. For meringue, in a medium mixing bowl dissolve ¾ cup sugar in the boiling water. Cool to room temperature. Add the meringue powder. Beat on low speed until combined; beat on high speed until stiff peaks form (tips stand straight). By hand, fold 3 tablespoons of the crushed candy into the meringue. Spread meringue over chocolate sauce layer, sealing to edge. Sprinkle top with remaining crushed candy. Freeze until firm (several hours or overnight). Bake in a 475°F oven for 3 to 4 minutes or just until meringue is lightly browned. Cover loosely and return to freezer for a few hours or overnight before serving. Makes 8 servings.

Apple Dumplings

1¾ cups water
1¼ cups sugar
½ teaspoon ground cinnamon
½ teaspoon ground nutmeg
 Several drops red food coloring
 (optional)
2 tablespoons butter
2¼ cups all-purpose flour
¼ teaspoon salt

⅔ cup shortening
6 to 8 tablespoons water
6 small cooking apples (about 1½
 pounds), such as Granny Smith,
 Rome Beauty, Braeburn, or Gala
 Sweetened whipped cream (optional)
 Maraschino cherries (optional)
 Vanilla ice cream (optional)

1. For syrup, in a medium saucepan combine the 1¾ cups water, 1 cup of the sugar, ¼ teaspoon of the cinnamon, ¼ teaspoon of the nutmeg, and, if desired, the food coloring. Heat to boiling; reduce heat. Simmer, uncovered, for 10 minutes or until syrup is reduced to 1½ cups. Remove saucepan from heat; stir in the butter.

2. Meanwhile, for pastry, combine flour and salt. Cut in shortening until pieces are pea-size. Add the 6 to 8 tablespoons water, a tablespoon at a time, mixing until flour mixture is moistened. Form dough into a ball. On a lightly floured surface, roll dough into an 18×12-inch rectangle; cut into six 6-inch squares.

3. Peel and core apples. Place an apple on each pastry square. Combine the remaining ¼ cup sugar, ¼ teaspoon cinnamon, and ¼ teaspoon nutmeg; sprinkle over fruit. Moisten edges of pastry with water; fold corners to center over fruit. Pinch pastry corners together to seal. Place dumplings in a 13×9×2-inch baking pan. Pour syrup into pan around dumplings.

4. Bake, uncovered, in a 375°F oven for 40 to 45 minutes or until fruit is tender and pastry is golden. To serve, spoon syrup over dumplings. If desired, top with sweetened whipped cream and a maraschino cherry, and serve with ice cream. Makes 6 servings.

When retired Test Kitchen home economist Jean Brekke talks about her favorite recipes, we listen. That's because Jean worked in the Test Kitchen in the '40s, then again in the '60s, '70s and '80s—she's seen a lot of good food over the years. This homespun dessert, which was already considered wonderfully old-fashioned when it was published in the 1953 edition of the *New Cook Book*, ranks as one of Jean's top picks. Hint: You don't have to use the red food coloring; it's very '50s, we admit, but it adds a little color to the sauce.

"What's not to like?" That's the general consensus on this cookie, with its buttery-rich shortbread crust and luscious topping of nuts and coconut that's similar in consistency to a pecan-pie filling. The recipe won the Prize Tested Recipe contest in September 1959.

Coconut Diamonds

6 tablespoons butter or margarine, softened	1 teaspoon vanilla
¼ cup granulated sugar	1 cup brown sugar
¼ teaspoon salt	2 tablespoons all-purpose flour
1 cup sifted all-purpose flour	¼ teaspoon salt
2 eggs	1 cup flaked coconut
	½ cup coarsely chopped walnuts

1. In a medium mixing bowl beat butter with an electric mixer on medium to high speed for 30 seconds. Add the granulated sugar and ¼ teaspoon salt. Stir in the 1 cup flour. Pat mixture onto bottom of a 9×9×2-inch baking pan. Bake in a 350°F oven for 15 minutes or until lightly browned.

2. Meanwhile, beat eggs slightly; add vanilla. Gradually add the brown sugar, beating just until blended. Add the 2 tablespoons flour and ¼ teaspoon salt. Stir in coconut and walnuts. Spread over baked layer. Bake about 20 minutes more or until top appears set; cool. Cut into diamonds. Store, covered, in refrigerator. Makes 18.

Pecan Crispies

½ cup shortening	¼ teaspoon salt
½ cup butter	2 eggs
2½ cups packed brown sugar	2½ cups all-purpose flour
½ teaspoon baking soda	1 cup chopped pecans

1. In a large mixing bowl beat the shortening and butter with an electric mixer on medium to high speed for 30 seconds. Add the brown sugar, baking soda, and salt; beat until mixture is combined, scraping sides of bowl occasionally. Beat in eggs until combined. Beat in as much of the flour as you can with the mixer. Stir in any remaining flour with a wooden spoon. Stir in pecans.

2. Drop dough by rounded teaspoons about 2 inches apart onto a greased cookie sheet. Bake in a 350°F oven about 12 minutes or until lightly browned and edges are set.* Makes 60 crispies.

*Note: For cookies with a chewier center and crisp edges, bake for only 10 minutes.

Myrna Johnston is somewhat of a *Better Homes and Gardens* legend. Not only was she the magazine's food editor for 33 years, but she was a key editor on early versions of our famous "red plaid" cookbook. Legend has it that whenever Myrna wanted cookies for a special occasion, this was the recipe she'd have the Test Kitchen prepare. The simple buttery, nutty cookie certainly deserves a place in our cookie hall of fame.

Who doesn't love chocolate and brownies? Perhaps that's why we have more than 100 brownie recipes in our archives. This greatest hit, from 1963, boasts three delectable layers—a chewy oatmeal cookie crust, a fudgy layer, and a creamy frosting—for one solid-gold treat.

Trilevel Brownies

1	cup quick-cooking rolled oats	1	ounce unsweetened chocolate, melted and cooled
½	cup all-purpose flour	1	teaspoon vanilla
½	cup packed brown sugar	¼	teaspoon baking powder
¼	teaspoon baking soda	½	cup chopped walnuts
½	cup butter, melted	1	ounce unsweetened chocolate
1	egg	2	tablespoons butter
¾	cup granulated sugar	1½	cups sifted powdered sugar
⅔	cup all-purpose flour	½	teaspoon vanilla
¼	cup milk		Walnut halves (optional)
¼	cup butter, melted		

1. For the bottom layer, stir together oats, the ½ cup flour, the brown sugar, and baking soda. Stir in the ½ cup melted butter. Pat mixture into the bottom of an ungreased 11×7×1½-inch baking pan. Bake in a 350°F oven for 10 minutes.

2. Meanwhile, for the middle layer, stir together the egg, granulated sugar, the ⅔ cup flour, the milk, the ¼ cup melted butter, the 1 ounce melted chocolate, the 1 teaspoon vanilla, and the baking powder until smooth. Fold in chopped walnuts. Spread batter evenly over baked layer in pan. Bake 25 minutes more. Place on a wire rack while preparing top layer.

3. For the top layer, in a medium saucepan heat and stir the 1 ounce chocolate and the 2 tablespoons butter until melted. Stir in the powdered sugar and the ½ teaspoon vanilla. Stir in enough hot water (1 to 2 tablespoons) to make a mixture that is almost pourable. Spread over brownies. If desired, garnish with walnut halves. Cool in pan on wire rack. Cut into bars. Makes 24 brownies.

In honor of the Test Kitchen's 30th anniversary, the September 1959 edition of Better Homes and Gardens Magazine *allowed a sneak peek behind the kitchen doors.*

Four Test Kitchens in one! Come on in and meet the staff

WE'RE PROUD of our Test Kitchen staff. All are graduate home economists who are expert cooks. After a day of recipe testing, all go home and fix a good dinner for lucky husbands.

These technicians develop and perfect recipes, of course. But they also test new products so we can tell you about them in "These Foods are News!" And they cook and arrange foods for dress rehearsals before photographs are taken.

The big room you see in the picture is divided into four kitchens, each planned exactly like a home kitchen—with a technician in charge. Some of the ranges and refrigerators are gas, others electric—we test with both.

An almost constant parade of new equipment comes to the Test Kitchens to replace the older models—from dishwashers to electric can openers. Revolutionary equipment—like the electronic range—is given a practical tryout.

Photographs: Hopkins

71

Foods and Equipment Editor Myrna Johnston says tasting is fun—and a job!

She's the little lady in the brown suit. A graduate home economist herself, and a wife and mother, she has directed the editorial staff of home economists for over 22 years.

Hugh Curtis, editor of *Better Homes & Gardens*, joins the taste panel.

Every food the technicians prepare is scored by the taste panel for family appeal—practicality—and downright deliciousness.

To be published, a recipe must meet our high standards and merit the faith of our readers.

Whether you tote it to a tailgate, pass it at a potluck, or offer it at the office, everyone's going to love you for sharing this caramely, nutty, buttery, crunchy delight. It's irresistible. What? You don't own a candy thermometer? There's never been a better reason to buy one.

Caramel Crunch Corn

8	cups popped popcorn	1	cup butter
1	cup pecan halves, toasted	½	cup light-color corn syrup
1	cup slivered almonds, toasted	1	teaspoon vanilla
1⅓	cups sugar		

1. Remove all unpopped kernels from popped popcorn. Place popcorn and nuts in a 17×12×2-inch baking or roasting pan. Keep popcorn warm in a 300°F oven while making caramel mixture.

2. For the caramel mixture, butter sides of a heavy medium saucepan; in saucepan combine the sugar, butter, and corn syrup. Cook and stir over medium-high heat until mixture boils. Clip a candy thermometer to the side of the saucepan. Reduce heat to medium; continue boiling at a moderate, steady rate, stirring frequently, until the thermometer registers 280°F, soft-crack stage (about 15 minutes). Remove from heat; stir in vanilla. Carefully pour caramel mixture over popcorn mixture; stir gently to coat. Spread popcorn mixture on a large piece of buttered foil to cool. Quickly break into clusters with two forks. Store in a tightly covered container. Makes 15 servings.

Almond Butter Crunch

1 **cup butter**	7 **2.6-ounce milk chocolate bars, melted**
1⅓ **cups sugar**	1 **cup finely chopped blanched almonds, toasted**
1 **tablespoon light-color corn syrup**	
3 **tablespoons water**	
1 **cup coarsely chopped blanched almonds, toasted**	

1. Line a 13×9×2-inch baking pan with foil, extending foil over the edges of pan; set pan aside. Butter sides of a heavy 2-quart saucepan. In saucepan melt butter; add the sugar, corn syrup, and water. Cook and stir over medium-high heat until mixture boils. Clip a candy thermometer to side of pan. Reduce heat to medium; continue boiling at a moderate steady rate, stirring occasionally, until thermometer registers 290°F*, soft-crack stage (about 15 minutes). Quickly stir in coarsely chopped almonds; spread in prepared pan.

2. Cool toffee about 2 minutes or until set. Spread top with half the chocolate; sprinkle with half the finely chopped nuts. Chill for 15 to 20 minutes or until chocolate is firm. Cover with waxed paper; invert onto a baking sheet. Spread with the remaining chocolate. Sprinkle remaining almonds on chocolate. Chill until the chocolate is firm. Break in pieces. Makes 42 servings.

*Note: Watch carefully after temperature reaches 280°F.

"It's a triple treat of chocolate, toffee, and almonds," exclaimed the note originally published with the recipe in December 1961. Our home economists wondered how on earth this recipe got buried and forgotten over the years. It's a keeper—perhaps our best version of toffee ever!

This candy has a delightfully old-fashioned appeal. It's a little like a praline, but the dates and cherries bring an added sweet and fruity dimension. Hint: Be sure to combine the fruits and nuts as directed so the fruit doesn't clump together.

Caramelized Fruit and Nuts

1 cup packed brown sugar	½ cup walnut pieces
½ cup granulated sugar	½ cup pecan halves
½ cup milk	½ cup snipped pitted dates
1 tablespoon light-color corn syrup	½ cup candied cherries, halved
1 tablespoon butter	¼ cup blanched almonds, toasted
1 tablespoon vanilla	

1. Butter 2 baking sheets or line with waxed paper; set aside. Butter the sides of a heavy 1½-quart saucepan. In the saucepan combine the brown sugar, granulated sugar, milk, and corn syrup. Cook and stir over medium-high heat until sugars dissolve and mixture boils. Clip a candy thermometer to side of pan. Reduce heat to medium-low; continue boiling at a moderate, steady rate, stirring occasionally, until thermometer registers 236°F, soft-ball stage (10 to 15 minutes). Remove from heat. Add butter and vanilla, but do not stir. Cool, without stirring, to 150°F (about 20 minutes). Meanwhile combine walnuts, pecans, dates, cherries, and almonds.

2. Remove thermometer from saucepan. Beat mixture just until it thickens and begins to lose its gloss (3 to 4 minutes). Quickly stir in nut mixture until pieces are coated. Drop immediately from a teaspoon onto prepared baking sheets. Let stand until set (about 1 hour). Makes 24 candy clusters.

Almond Butter Crunch, page 77, Caramelized Fruit and Nuts, and Caramel Crunch Corn, page 76

1970

1977

It's true—soaring food costs and a recession hit home during the '70s. Yet while the practical side of our Test Kitchen helped budget-minded hardworking families beat the clock and cook on a shoestring, our fun-loving side tapped into the adventuresome spirit of those times. Come join the party with Frisky Sours, Smoky Cheese Ball, Swiss Fondue, and other enduring favorites of this anything-goes decade.

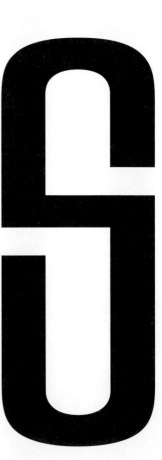

favorites from the

The '70s in our kitchen

1973: It figures that in the casual, go-with-the-flow '70s "entertaining" was out and "getting together" was in. This article, from the October 1973 issue of *Better Homes and Gardens* magazine, described a good time as "good company plus good food, not a spectacular production which suggests you've knocked yourself out in the kitchen." We've been helping hosts let the good times roll—without knocking themselves out in the kitchen—ever since.

1973

1970

1972

1970: This *Better Homes and Gardens* magazine cover, the first of the '70s, hinted at the economic challenges in the decade ahead. And while none of our editors particularly wants to take credit for the Hot Dog Soufflé that appeared during those years, we are proud of the many thrifty recipes we created to help cooks provide nourishing, satisfying meals for their families when money was tight.

1972: This article, featuring farmers' markets across America, reflected the era's passion for busting out of the kitchen and finding great food at its source. Our editors traveled far and wide, heading to family farms, homes, festivals, and food markets both in the United States and abroad—wherever good eating was to be found. Back in the Test Kitchen, our pros transformed the new discoveries into exciting, doable recipes for the home cook.

Rabbit Stew

HE COOKS

1978: With Mom returning to work and traditional gender roles going by the wayside, men began taking their turns in the kitchen. Throughout the decade, male readers sent us their favorite recipes— everything from a Burgundy-Basted Duckling to a Harvey Wallbanger Cake—which we tested and perfected for the popular "He Cooks" column in *Better Homes and Gardens* magazine.

1978

1970s: Here's a look at a 1972 taste panel in our Test Kitchen, fondly remembered as The Blue Kitchen before it was remodeled in the late '70s. Our Test Kitchen seal ensured that every recipe had been tested until it met "high standards of family appeal, practicality, and deliciousness."

1970s

1977

1977: Though convenience cooking was alive and well during the '70s, the decade also saw a "scratch renaissance," when cooks tried their hands at making foods the old-fashioned way. Readers also became more and more curious about food in general, wanting to learn about new techniques and ingredients, not just out of necessity, but also for fun. Hobby cooks arrived on the culinary scene en masse, and we showed them how to do everything from tempering chocolate and salt curing a ham to making phyllo dough and bagels.

WHEN YOU look through the pages of *Better Homes and Gardens* from the 1970s, you see a lot of parties on those pages! There's no doubt about it—people in the '70s knew how to have a good time. These frisky little highballs will help you tap into the spirit of those years.

Frisky Sours

¾ cup frozen lemonade concentrate, thawed

⅓ cup frozen grapefruit juice concentrate, thawed

⅓ cup frozen orange juice concentrate, thawed

1½ cups whiskey

1½ cups cold water

Crushed ice

1. In a blender container combine juice concentrates, whiskey, and water. Cover and blend until frothy. Serve over crushed ice. Makes 8 (4-ounce) servings.

Orange-Eggnog Punch

1 **quart dairy eggnog, chilled**
1 **6-ounce can frozen orange juice**
    concentrate, thawed
1 **1-liter bottle lemon-lime carbonated**
    beverage, chilled

1 **pint vanilla ice cream**
    Ground nutmeg (optional)

1. In a punch bowl combine eggnog and orange juice concentrate. Slowly add carbonated beverage. Top with scoops of vanilla ice cream. Sprinkle with nutmeg, if desired. Makes 20 (4-ounce) servings.

WE LIKED the way the orange and vanilla ice cream reminded us of a childhood favorite flavor combination. We liked this punch even more when we spiked individual servings of it with a little Grand Marnier liqueur. If that sounds good to you, set a bottle of the orange-flavored brandy by the punch bowl. That way, those who don't care to imbibe can keep the treat nonalcoholic.

Smoky Cheese Ball

2	8-ounce packages cream cheese	2	tablespoons milk
2	cups finely shredded smoked cheddar,	2	teaspoons steak sauce
	Swiss, or Gouda cheese	1	cup finely chopped nuts, toasted
½	cup butter or margarine		Assorted crackers

1. Place the cream cheese, shredded cheese, and butter in a large bowl and let stand at room temperature for 30 minutes. Add milk and steak sauce; beat until fluffy. Cover and chill for 4 to 24 hours.

2. Shape cheese mixture into a ball; roll in nuts. Let cheese ball stand for 15 minutes before serving. Serve with crackers. Makes 3½ cups spread.

Make-ahead directions: Prepare as above, except do not roll in nuts. Wrap cheese ball in moisture- and vapor-proof plastic wrap. Freeze for up to 1 month. To serve, thaw in refrigerator overnight. Roll in nuts. Let stand for 30 minutes at room temperature before serving.

"CHRISTMAS wouldn't be Christmas at my house without this delicious cheese ball," says Maryellyn Krantz, 30-year veteran of the Test Kitchen. While this ever-popular classic needed little updating since it first appeared in 1972, a recent discovery was how well it freezes! If you're hosting a small party, divide it into two balls, and freeze the extra one for your next small gathering.

Cheese Puffs

1   3-ounce package cream cheese,
      softened
1   egg yolk
1   teaspoon lemon juice
1   teaspoon snipped fresh chives
      Dash black pepper
½   cup shredded white cheddar cheese
      (2 ounces)

2   slices bacon, crisp-cooked, drained,
      and crumbled
1   17.3-ounce package (2 sheets) frozen
      puff pastry, thawed
     Milk

1. For filling, in a small mixing bowl combine the cream cheese, egg yolk, lemon juice, chives, and pepper; beat with an electric mixer on medium speed until nearly smooth. Stir in cheddar cheese and bacon.

2. On a lightly floured surface, roll 1 of the pastry sheets into a 12-inch square. Cut into sixteen 3-inch squares. Top each square with about 1 teaspoon of the filling. Brush pastry edges with milk. Fold in half diagonally. Seal edges by pressing with tines of a fork or fingers. Place on an ungreased baking sheet. Repeat with remaining pastry sheet and filling. (If desired, cover and chill for up to 4 hours before baking.) Bake in a 400°F oven for 12 to 15 minutes or until golden brown. Serve warm. Makes 32 puffs.

THESE FLAKY morsels have always boasted a savory filling accented with cheddar cheese and crisp-cooked bacon. However, when the treats were first developed in 1974, they were made with purchased frozen patty shells. As soon as purchased puff pastry became widely available, we took full advantage to make these classics better than ever!

Swiss Fondue

3 cups shredded Gruyère or Swiss cheese (12 ounces)	1½ cups dry white wine
2 cups shredded Emmentaler, Gruyère, or Swiss cheese (8 ounces)	¼ cup milk
3 tablespoons all-purpose flour	2 tablespoons kirsch or dry sherry
12 1-inch slices herb bread or French bread, cut into 1-inch cubes, and/or broccoli or cauliflower florets	⅛ teaspoon ground nutmeg
	⅛ teaspoon white pepper
	Paprika (optional)

It Figures that the fondue craze really took off in the 1970s—the hassle-free style of entertaining fit right into the easygoing nature of that decade. Happily, the dish is making a spirited comeback these days, as a new generation discovers what fun it is to gather around the old flame. This recipe melds nutty-sweet Emmentaler and smooth-melting Gruyère with cherry-flavored brandy for a classic, crowd-pleasing version.

1. Let shredded cheeses stand at room temperature for 30 minutes. Toss cheeses with flour; set aside.

2. Meanwhile, place bread cubes on a baking sheet and bake in a 350°F oven for 5 to 7 minutes or until crisp and toasted; set aside. In a saucepan bring a small amount of water to boiling; add broccoli or cauliflower florets. Simmer, covered, about 3 minutes or until crisp-tender. Drain and rinse with cold water; set aside.

3. In a large saucepan heat wine over medium heat until small bubbles rise to the surface. Just before wine boils, reduce heat to low and stir in the cheese mixture, a little at a time, stirring constantly and making sure cheese is melted before adding more. Stir until the mixture bubbles gently.

4. Stir in milk, kirsch, nutmeg, and white pepper. Transfer cheese mixture to a fondue pot. Keep mixture bubbling gently over a fondue burner. (If mixture becomes too thick, stir in a little more milk.) If desired, sprinkle with paprika. Serve with toasted bread cubes and/or florets. Makes 12 servings.

Our Favorite Quiche Lorraine

Pastry for Single-Crust Pie
8 **slices bacon**
1 **medium onion, thinly sliced**
4 **beaten eggs**
1 **cup half-and-half or light cream**
1 **cup milk**
¼ **teaspoon salt**

Dash ground nutmeg
1½ **cups shredded Swiss cheese**
    (6 ounces)
1 **tablespoon all-purpose flour**
    Tomato wedges
    Fresh parsley

QUICHE WAS all over the place in the '70s—and it didn't take long before our Test Kitchen was all over the recipe. And while we've published some wonderful versions of the French egg pie over the years, this version of Quiche Lorraine may well be our gold standard. Taste this and you'll understand what the craze was all about!

1. Prepare Pastry for Single-Crust Pie. Line the unpricked pastry shell with a double thickness of heavy foil. Bake in a 450°F oven for 8 minutes. Remove foil. Bake for 4 to 5 minutes more or until pastry is set and dry. Remove from oven. Reduce oven temperature to 325°F. (Pie shell should still be hot when filling is added; do not partially bake pastry shell ahead of time.)

2. Meanwhile, in a large skillet cook bacon until crisp. Drain, reserving 2 tablespoons drippings. Finely crumble bacon; set aside. Cook sliced onion in reserved drippings over medium heat until tender but not brown; drain.

3. In a medium bowl stir together the eggs, half-and-half, milk, salt, and nutmeg. Stir in the crumbled bacon and onion. Toss together shredded cheese and flour. Add to egg mixture; mix well.

4. Pour egg mixture into the hot, baked pastry shell. Bake in the 325°F oven for 50 to 60 minutes or until a knife inserted near the center comes out clean. If necessary, cover edge of crust with foil to prevent overbrowning. Let stand 10 minutes. Garnish with tomatoes and parsley before serving. Makes 6 servings.

Pastry for a Single-Crust Pie: In a medium bowl stir together 1¼ cups all-purpose flour and ¼ teaspoon salt. Using a pastry blender, cut in ⅓ cup shortening until pieces are pea-size. Sprinkle 1 tablespoon of cold water over part of the flour mixture; gently toss with a fork. Push moistened dough to the side of the bowl. Repeat moistening flour mixture, 1 tablespoon at a time, until all is moistened (use 4 or 5 tablespoons total). Form dough into a ball. On a lightly floured surface, use your hands to slightly flatten dough. Roll dough from center to edges into a circle about 12 inches in diameter. To transfer pastry, wrap it around the rolling pin. Unroll pastry into a quiche dish or 9-inch pie plate. Ease pastry into pie plate, being careful not to stretch pastry. Trim pastry to ½ inch beyond edge of pie plate. Fold under extra pastry. Crimp edge as desired. Do not prick pastry. Bake as directed.

leftovers may not be the most glamorous topic in food today, but what can we say? We love this recipe! This cheese-topped pie, with its "crust" of stuffing, is one of the most satisfying ways to use leftover turkey that we've ever published.

Turkey Skillet Pie

1/3 cup chopped celery	Dash black pepper
6 tablespoons butter or margarine	3 cups finely chopped or ground cooked turkey*
2/3 cup water	
2 cups herb-seasoned stuffing mix	1 cup shredded Swiss cheese (4 ounces)
3 beaten eggs	
1 5-ounce can evaporated milk (2/3 cup)	2 tablespoons snipped fresh parsley
2 tablespoons finely chopped onion	1 1/2 cups leftover turkey gravy or one 12-ounce jar roasted turkey gravy

1. In a large skillet cook celery in butter until tender. Add water and stuffing mix; toss to coat. Set aside.

2. In a bowl combine the eggs, evaporated milk, onion, and pepper. Stir in turkey. Spoon turkey mixture into a well-greased 8-inch skillet; sprinkle with cheese. Top with stuffing mixture. Cook, covered, over medium-low heat for 10 to 15 minutes or until instant-read thermometer registers 160°F when inserted into center. Sprinkle with parsley. Let stand 5 minutes. Heat turkey gravy; serve over wedges of Turkey Skillet Pie. Makes 6 servings.

*Note: Do not use deli-style turkey.

German Meatballs with Spaetzle

1	slightly beaten egg	½	cup chopped onion
¼	cup milk	1	8-ounce carton dairy sour cream
¼	cup fine dry bread crumbs	2	tablespoons all-purpose flour
1	tablespoon snipped fresh parsley	½	to 1 teaspoon caraway seeds
½	teaspoon salt	2	cups all-purpose flour
	Dash black pepper	1	teaspoon salt
1	pound ground beef	2	slightly beaten eggs
1⅓	cups beef broth	1	cup milk
1	4-ounce can mushroom pieces and stems, drained		Snipped fresh parsley (optional)

1. In a large bowl combine the 1 egg, the ¼ cup milk, the fine dry bread crumbs, the 1 tablespoon parsley, the ½ teaspoon salt, and pepper; add ground meat and mix well. Shape mixture into twenty-four 1½-inch meatballs. In a large nonstick skillet brown meatballs; drain off fat. Add broth, mushrooms, and onion. Simmer, covered, for 20 minutes or until an instant-read thermometer inserted into meatballs registers 160°F. In a small bowl combine sour cream, the 2 tablespoons flour, and the caraway seeds; stir into broth. Cook and stir until mixture thickens and bubbles. Cook and stir 1 minute more.

2. For spaetzle, in a medium bowl combine the 2 cups flour and the 1 teaspoon salt. Add the remaining 2 eggs and the 1 cup milk; beat well. Let rest 5 to 10 minutes. Meanwhile, bring a large Dutch oven or kettle of salted water to boiling. Holding a coarse-sieved colander (such as the basket for a deep-fat fryer) over rapidly boiling water, pour batter into colander. Press batter through colander with back of wooden spoon or rubber spatula. Cook and stir 5 minutes; drain. Sprinkle with snipped parsley, if desired. Serve meatballs over spaetzle. Makes 4 to 6 servings.

IF YOU'RE hankering for comfort food, but want something a little off the beaten path, try this hearty, home-style recipe. What? You've never made pasta from scratch? Consider spaetzle a good place to start. These chewy homemade egg noodles are easy to make and worth the effort.

Borsch-Style Casserole

2	pounds beef short ribs	1½	teaspoons sugar
1	tablespoon cooking oil	1½	teaspoons vinegar
½	cup sliced celery (2 stalks)	1	cup fresh beet strips (1)
½	cup sliced onion	1	cup ½-inch carrot slices (2)
3	cups water	¾	cup bite-size turnip strips (1)
⅓	cup tomato paste	½	small head cabbage, cut into
1	teaspoon salt		4 wedges
⅛	teaspoon black pepper		Dairy sour cream
½	cup water		

1. Trim the fat from the ribs. In a 4-quart Dutch oven or kettle, brown ribs in hot oil. Drain off fat. Add the celery and onion. In a large bowl combine the 3 cups water, tomato paste, the 1 teaspoon salt, and the ⅛ teaspoon pepper; pour over vegetables in Dutch oven. Cover and bake in a 350°F oven for 2½ hours.

2. Skim off fat. Combine the remaining ½ cup water, the sugar, and vinegar; add to meat mixture. Add beet strips, carrot slices, and turnip strips; place cabbage wedges on vegetable mixture, pushing them partially into liquid. Cover and continue baking 1 hour more. Season to taste with additional salt and pepper. Spoon sour cream over each serving. Makes 4 servings.

FOOD TRENDS may come and go, but, as retired food editor Doris Eby notes, good food ideas never go away for long. After the recession hit in 1973, we appreciated short ribs because they were economical. Today, the cut often stars in clever braised dishes on trendy bistro menus. This borsch-style braise is definitely back in style.

PRIZE WINNING RECIPES FROM THRIFTY COOKS

by Doris Eby

Our Budget Recipe Contest brought in an avalanche of excellent entries—a gratifying response but tough on the judges who had to pick the ten top prizewinners and 100 honorable mentions. Once you try the ten top recipes, we think you'll give them your dinner-bell-ringing endorsement.

Buying information, page 103

$1000 Prizewinner

BORSCH-STYLE CASSEROLE

Mrs. Huguette Griffith, of Charlotte, North Carolina, our first prize winner, recommended Borsch-style Casserole as a real man-pleaser—and we agree! Economical short ribs simmer in a superlative broth with lots of vitamin-packed vegetables— the sometimes forgotten ones like turnips, beets, and cabbage that always used to find their way into grandmother's stewpot.

A little sugar and vinegar give the stew tang.

To make this blue-ribbon winner company special, top each serving with a dollop of sour cream and accompany with black bread and frosty mugs of cold beer.

2 pounds beef short ribs, cut up
1 tablespoon cooking oil
2 cups sliced carrots (4 carrots)
1½ cups turnip strips (3 turnips)
1 cup sliced celery (3 stalks celery)

1 cup sliced onion (1 onion)
4 cups water
1 6-ounce can tomato paste
1 tablespoon salt
¼ teaspoon pepper
1 cup water
1 tablespoon sugar
1 tablespoon vinegar
2 cups fresh beet strips (2 beets)
1 small head cabbage, cut in 6 wedges
Dairy sour cream

In 4½-quart Dutch oven, brown ribs in hot oil. Drain off excess fat. Add carrot, turnip, celery, and onion. Blend together the 4 cups water, the tomato paste, salt, and pepper; pour over vegetables in Dutch oven. Cover and bake in 350° oven for 2 hours. Skim off fat. Combine remaining 1 cup water, the sugar, and vinegar; add to meat mixture. Add beet strips and place cabbage wedges atop mixture, pushing partially into liquid. Cover and continue baking 1½ hours more. Pass sour cream to spoon atop each serving. Makes 6 servings.

BETTER HOMES AND GARDENS, FEBRUARY, 1975

IN NOVEMBER 1970, our magazine ran a recipe contest for "Your Favorite Man's Favorite Recipe." Nancy Byal, a food editor at the time, remembers the contest well—they received over 80,000 entries. While we'd likely not run such a gender-specific contest these days, we can't help being touched by the outpouring of responses. It shows once again that cooking is often about more than getting food on the table——it's a simple everyday token of love. Share this nourishing, stick-to-your-ribs homemade soup—which took second prize in the contest—with someone special in your life soon.

Hearty Hodgepodge

6 slices bacon	3 cups cubed potatoes (4 medium)
1 medium onion, thinly sliced	1 clove garlic, minced
1 pound crosscut beef shanks	1 4-ounce link fully cooked Polish
¾ pound ham hock	sausage, thinly sliced
6 cups water	Toasted and buttered French bread
½ teaspoon salt	
2 15-ounce cans garbanzo beans,	
rinsed and drained	

1. In a 4- to 6-quart Dutch oven, cook bacon until crisp; drain, reserving 2 tablespoons drippings. Crumble bacon and refrigerate. Add sliced onion to reserved drippings in pan. Cook until tender. Add beef shanks, ham hock, water, and salt.

2. Heat to boiling; reduce heat. Simmer, covered, for 1½ hours or until beef is tender. Remove beef shanks from broth. Remove meat from beef shanks and ham hock and cut up; discard bones. Carefully skim fat from broth. Return cut up meat to broth; add beans, potatoes, and garlic. Return to boiling; reduce heat. Simmer, covered, for 30 minutes more. Add sausage and simmer, covered, 15 minutes more. Stir in bacon. Serve with toasted French bread. Makes 8 servings.

Spaghetti Pie

4 ounces dried spaghetti	1 clove garlic, minced
1 tablespoon butter or margarine	1 8-ounce can tomato sauce
1 egg, beaten	1 teaspoon dried oregano, crushed
¼ cup grated Parmesan cheese	Nonstick cooking spray
8 ounces ground beef	1 cup low-fat cottage cheese, drained
½ cup chopped onion (1 medium)	½ cup shredded part-skim mozzarella
½ cup chopped green sweet pepper	cheese (2 ounces)
½ teaspoon fennel seeds, crushed	

1. Cook spaghetti according to package directions; drain. Return spaghetti to warm saucepan. Stir butter into hot spaghetti until melted. Stir in egg and Parmesan cheese; set aside.

2. Meanwhile, in a medium skillet cook the ground beef, onion, sweet pepper, fennel seeds, and garlic until meat is brown and onion is tender. Drain off fat. Stir in tomato sauce and oregano; heat through.

3. Coat a 9-inch pie plate with nonstick cooking spray. Press spaghetti mixture onto bottom and up sides of pie plate to form a crust. Spread cottage cheese on the crust, spreading it up the sides. Spread meat mixture over cottage cheese. Sprinkle with shredded mozzarella cheese. Bake in a 350°F oven for 20 to 25 minutes or until bubbly and heated through. To serve, cut into wedges. Makes 6 servings.

ALL-TIME-FAVORITE

recipes are sometimes deemed as such because our Test Kitchen staff love them and because their families do too. This hearty, home-style dish ranks as a top favorite of Maryellyn Krantz's husband, John. Hint: To form the crust, use a large wooden spoon or a rubber spatula to press the spaghetti onto the bottom and up the sides of the pie plate.

Cassoulet-Style Stew

8 ounces dry navy beans	1/4 cup dry red wine or beef broth
3 cups water	1 1/4 teaspoons salt
1 meaty lamb shank (1 to 1 1/2 pounds)	1 tablespoon snipped fresh thyme or
1 tablespoon olive oil or cooking oil	1 teaspoon dried thyme, crushed
1 cup chopped celery (including leaves)	2 teaspoons snipped fresh rosemary or
1 medium potato, peeled and coarsely	1/2 teaspoon dried rosemary,
chopped	crushed
1/2 cup coarsely chopped peeled carrot	1/4 teaspoon black pepper
1/2 cup coarsely chopped peeled parsnip	1 14 1/2-ounce can diced tomatoes,
2 cloves garlic, minced	drained
3 1/2 cups water	Fresh rosemary or thyme sprigs
1 1/2 cups sliced fresh mushrooms	(optional)
2/3 cup dry black-eyed peas, rinsed and	
drained	

1. Rinse beans. In a Dutch oven combine beans and the 3 cups water. Bring to boiling; reduce heat. Simmer, uncovered, for 2 minutes. Remove from heat. Cover and let stand for 1 hour. (Or place beans in water in a Dutch oven. Cover and let stand in a cool place for 6 to 8 hours or overnight.) Drain and rinse beans.

2. In a 4- to 5-quart Dutch oven or kettle brown lamb shank in hot oil over medium-high heat. Add celery, potato, carrot, parsnip, and garlic. Cook over medium-high heat for 5 minutes, stirring frequently. Add the 3 1/2 cups water, mushrooms, black-eyed peas, wine, salt, dried thyme (if using), dried rosemary (if using), pepper, and beans. Bring to boiling; reduce heat. Simmer, covered, about 1 1/2 hours or until the beans and peas are tender. Remove shank; let cool.

3. Remove meat from shank; chop meat. Stir meat, tomatoes, fresh thyme (if using), and fresh rosemary (if using) into bean mixture. Return to boiling; reduce heat. Simmer, covered, for 15 minutes more. To serve, ladle stew into bowls. If desired, garnish with fresh rosemary or thyme sprigs. Makes 6 servings.

Make-ahead directions: Prepare stew as directed. Let cool for 30 minutes. Place stew in freezer containers and freeze for up to 3 months. To serve, place frozen stew in a saucepan. Heat, covered, over medium-low heat about 45 minutes or until heated through, stirring occasionally to break stew mixture apart.

TEST KITCHEN Director Lynn Blanchard ranks this stew among her favorites. "It uses lamb shanks, which has always been a favorite meal of mine," Lynn says. The full-flavored stew—based on a classic French dish—is perfect for casual entertaining because its slow simmering allows the cook plenty of time to relax and converse with guests.

HERE'S AN IDEA—why not host a '70s party? Start with the Smoky Cheese Ball, page 86. Then move onto these boldly flavored he-man steaks, hot off the grill, served with Vera Cruz Tomatoes, page 105. Have the Banana Split Cake, page 110, waiting in the wings for dessert. And of course, don't forget to raise a glass to the fun food of that decade with a round of Frisky Sours, page 84.

Onion-Stuffed Steak

4 6- to 8-ounce boneless beef top loin steaks, cut ¾ to 1 inch thick	¼ teaspoon black pepper
1½ cups chopped onion	¼ cup dry red wine
4 cloves garlic, minced	2 tablespoons soy sauce
¼ cup butter or margarine	1 8-ounce package fresh mushrooms, quartered (3 cups)
¼ teaspoon celery salt	¼ cup butter or margarine

1. Slice a pocket in one side of each steak, cutting almost, but not all the way, to the other side; set aside.

2. In a large skillet cook the onion and garlic in ¼ cup hot butter until the onion is tender. Stir in the celery salt and pepper. Stuff pockets with onion mixture; skewer closed. Mix wine and soy sauce; brush on steaks.

3. Grill steaks directly over medium coals until desired doneness, turning once halfway through grilling. (Allow 12 to 14 minutes for medium rare [145°F]. Check for doneness using an instant-read meat thermometer.) Meanwhile, in a large skillet cook the mushrooms in the remaining ¼ cup butter until tender. Serve steaks with mushrooms. Makes 4 servings.

Farm-Style Green Beans

4 thick slices bacon, cut up	½ teaspoon salt
2 medium onions, sliced	1 pound green beans, washed,
3 medium tomatoes, peeled, seeded,	stemmed, and cut up (4 cups)
and chopped (2 cups)	

1. In a large skillet cook bacon until crisp. Remove bacon, reserving 3 tablespoons drippings. Drain bacon and set aside. Cook the onions in the reserved drippings over medium heat until onions are tender. Add the tomatoes and salt; cook, uncovered, for 5 minutes more or until most of the liquid is absorbed.

2. Meanwhile, in a medium saucepan cook the beans in a small amount of boiling salted water for 10 to 15 minutes or until crisp-tender; drain. Transfer beans to a serving bowl. Top beans with the tomato mixture and bacon pieces. Makes 8 servings.

THIS RECIPE was published in a 1976 *Better Homes and Gardens* magazine story that featured specialities from the tables of Wisconsin dairy farmers. Try it in the summer, when fresh green beans and homegrown tomatoes are in season, and you'll understand why it ranks as one of the best ways ever to prepare green beans.

Green Beans Parmesan

1　16-ounce package frozen French-style green beans
¼　cup chopped onion
2　tablespoons butter or margarine
2　tablespoons all-purpose flour
½　teaspoon salt
1¼　cups milk

¼　cup grated Parmesan cheese
1　8-ounce can sliced water chestnuts, drained
¾　cup soft bread crumbs
2　tablespoons butter or margarine, melted

1. Cook beans in salted water according to package directions; drain. In a medium saucepan cook onion in 2 tablespoons butter until tender; stir in flour and salt. Stir in milk all at once; cook and stir until thickened and bubbly. Stir in half the Parmesan cheese. Stir in the cooked beans and water chestnuts; turn into a 1-quart casserole.

2. Toss the remaining Parmesan cheese with crumbs and melted butter; sprinkle on bean mixture in casserole. Bake, uncovered, in a 350°F oven about 30 minutes or until bubbly. Makes 6 to 8 servings.

IF YOU FEEL you've "bean" there, done that with classic green bean casserole (the one with canned fried onions on the top), try this rich and creamy gourmet version. The "wow, what is it" factor is the crisp water chestnuts studded throughout.

Belgian Creamed Potatoes

4	cups thinly sliced potatoes	2	tablespoons butter or margarine
1	cup sliced leeks	¾	cup shredded Swiss cheese
½	teaspoon salt		(3 ounces)
¾	cup whipping cream		

1. In a 1½-quart casserole, combine potatoes, leeks, and salt. Add whipping cream; dot with butter. Bake, covered, in a 350°F oven for 30 minutes. Uncover and gently stir. Bake for 25 to 30 minutes more or until potatoes are tender. Sprinkle with cheese; bake 5 minutes more or until cheese is melted. Makes 6 servings.

SOME PEOPLE might call these au gratin potatoes; we call them amazing. Leeks bring a mellow flavor, and the method is much easier than many au gratin potato recipes that we've come across over the years. Consider it a terrific and easy dinner party side dish.

Vera Cruz Tomatoes

4 **medium tomatoes**	½ **cup dairy sour cream**
3 **strips bacon**	**Dash bottled hot pepper sauce**
¼ **cup chopped onion**	½ **cup shredded mozzarella cheese**
8 **ounces fresh spinach, shredded**	**(2 ounces)**
(4 cups lightly packed)	**Salt**

1. Cut the top from each tomato, cutting a scallop edge ½ to 1 inch from the top. Use a spoon to scoop out tomato pulp. Set upside down on paper towels to drain. Meanwhile, in a 10-inch skillet cook bacon until crisp; drain, reserving 2 tablespoons drippings. Crumble bacon and set aside. Cook onion in reserved drippings over medium heat until tender; stir in spinach. Reduce heat to medium-low. Cook, covered, until spinach is wilted, 1 to 2 minutes. Remove from heat; stir in bacon, sour cream, hot pepper sauce, and half of the shredded cheese.

2. Turn tomatoes right side up; sprinkle with salt. Fill tomatoes with spinach mixture. Place in an 8×8×2-inch baking pan or dish. Bake, covered, in a 375°F oven for 10 to 15 minutes or until tomatoes are softened. Top with remaining shredded cheese; bake 5 minutes more. Serve warm. Makes 4 servings.

PICTURE bacon, spinach, sour cream, and mozzarella all stuffed inside a big red tomato. As someone noted at our taste panel, "What's not to like?" The editors in 1972 must have felt the same way; the recipe took the top award in the Fancy Summer Vegetables category in August of that year. We also noted that this "fancy" side dish would be great with a simple roast or grilled meat entrée.

Potato Bread with Sour Cream and Chives

6¼ to 6¾ cups all-purpose flour	1 10¾-ounce can condensed cream of potato soup
2 packages active dry yeast	
1½ cups milk	½ cup dairy sour cream
2 tablespoons sugar	¼ cup snipped fresh chives
2 tablespoons butter or margarine	1 teaspoon dried tarragon, crushed, or
2 teaspoons salt	1 teaspoon dried dill

1. In large mixing bowl combine 2½ cups of the all-purpose flour and the yeast. In a medium saucepan heat and stir the milk, sugar, butter, and salt just until warm (120°F to 130°F) and butter almost melts. Add milk mixture to flour mixture along with condensed soup, sour cream, chives, and tarragon. Beat with an electric mixer at low speed for 30 seconds, scraping sides of bowl constantly. Beat on high speed for 3 minutes. Using a wooden spoon, stir in as much of the remaining flour as you can.

2. Turn dough out onto a lightly floured surface. Knead in enough of the remaining flour to make a moderately stiff dough that is smooth and elastic (6 to 8 minutes total). Shape dough into a ball. Place in a lightly greased bowl, turning once to grease surface. Cover; let rise in a warm place until double (45 to 60 minutes).

3. Punch dough down. Cover; let rest 10 minutes. Meanwhile, lightly grease two 9×5×3-inch loaf pans. Divide dough in half; shape into 2 loaves. Place in prepared pans. Cover and let rise in a warm place until nearly double (30 to 40 minutes).

4. Bake in a 400°F oven for 20 to 25 minutes or until bread sounds hollow when lightly tapped. Immediately remove bread from pans. Cool bread on wire racks. Makes 2 loaves (32 servings).

TO QUALIFY as a "favorite," a recipe must—first and foremost—taste great. And if there's a shortcut trick involved, well, so much the better! Here, thanks to a can of soup, you can have a moist, light-textured potato bread without peeling, boiling, or mashing potatoes.

Rhubarb-Strawberry Coffee Cake

Rhubarb Filling

3	cups all-purpose flour
1	cup sugar
1	teaspoon baking soda
1	teaspoon baking powder
1	teaspoon salt
1	cup butter

2	slightly beaten eggs
1	cup buttermilk or sour milk*
1	teaspoon vanilla
½	cup sugar
½	cup all-purpose flour
¼	cup butter

1. Prepare Rhubarb Filling; set aside to cool. In a large bowl stir together the 3 cups flour, the 1 cup sugar, the baking soda, baking powder, and salt. Cut in the 1 cup butter until mixture resembles fine crumbs. In a small bowl combine the eggs, buttermilk, and vanilla; add to flour mixture. Stir to moisten.

2. Spread half the batter in a greased 13×9×2-inch baking pan. Spread cooled filling over batter in pan. Spoon remaining batter in small mounds over filling. In a small bowl combine the ½ cup sugar and the ½ cup flour. Cut in the ¼ cup butter until mixture resembles fine crumbs. Sprinkle crumb mixture over batter in pan. Bake in a 350°F oven for 40 to 45 minutes or until golden. Serve warm. Makes 12 to 16 servings.

Rhubarb Filling: In a medium saucepan combine 3 cups fresh rhubarb or one 16-ounce package frozen unsweetened sliced rhubarb, and 4 cups hulled fresh strawberries or one 16-ounce package frozen unsweetened whole strawberries, thawed and halved. Cook fruit, covered, about 5 minutes. Add 2 tablespoons lemon juice. Combine 1 cup sugar and ⅓ cup cornstarch; add to rhubarb mixture. Cook and stir 4 to 5 minutes until thickened and bubbly; cool.

*To make sour milk: For 1 cup sour milk, place 1 tablespoon lemon juice or vinegar in a glass measuring cup. Add enough milk to make 1 cup total liquid; stir. Let mixture stand for 5 minutes before using.

ONE THING Test Kitchen pros learn quickly is that there's no way to keep a good recipe to yourself. That is, if you bring in a terrific goodie from your personal recipe file, don't be surprised if a co-worker asks about publishing it! Case in point: Not too long after Marge Steenson shared this wonderful coffee cake with her colleagues in the Test Kitchen, it appeared in a *Better Homes and Gardens* magazine story.

comfort foods got a revival in the late '70s, and throughout that decade a back-to-basics movement was in full swing. It's no wonder this cake was so popular then. Serve it warm from the oven with a scoop of vanilla ice cream, and everyone around your table will truly feel treated to something special.

Oatmeal Cake

¼ cup butter	¼ teaspoon baking soda
1 egg	¼ teaspoon salt
⅔ cup boiling water	⅛ teaspoon ground nutmeg
½ cup rolled oats	⅓ cup granulated sugar
1 cup all-purpose flour	¼ cup packed brown sugar
1 teaspoon baking powder	½ teaspoon vanilla
½ teaspoon ground cinnamon	Broiled Nut Topping

1. Allow butter and egg to stand at room temperature for 30 minutes. Meanwhile, grease and lightly flour an 8×1½-inch round baking pan; set pan aside. In a small bowl pour boiling water over oats. Stir until combined; let stand 20 minutes. In another small bowl stir together the flour, baking powder, cinnamon, baking soda, salt, and nutmeg; set aside.

2. In a medium mixing bowl beat butter with an electric mixer on medium to high speed for 30 seconds. Add granulated sugar, brown sugar, and vanilla; beat until well combined. Add egg; beat until combined. Alternately add the flour mixture and oatmeal mixture to butter mixture, beating on low speed after each addition just until combined. Spread batter into prepared pan.

3. Bake in a 350°F oven about 25 minutes or until a wooden toothpick inserted near the center comes out clean. Cool cake in pan on a wire rack for 10 minutes. Remove from pan; invert onto a wire rack so top of cake is up. Cool at least 1 hour. Prepare Broiled Nut Topping.

4. Transfer cake to a baking sheet. Spread Broiled Nut Topping over cake. Broil about 4 inches from heat for 2 to 3 minutes or until topping is bubbly and golden. Cool on a wire rack before serving. Makes 6 to 8 servings.

Broiled Nut Topping: In a small saucepan combine 3 tablespoons butter and 1 tablespoon half-and-half, light cream, or milk. Cook and stir until butter melts. Add ⅓ cup packed brown sugar; stir until sugar dissolves. Remove from heat. Stir in ⅔ cup chopped pecans or walnuts and ¼ cup flaked coconut.

Pumpkin Cake Roll

3	eggs	1	cup granulated sugar
¾	cup all-purpose flour	⅔	cup canned pumpkin
2	teaspoons ground cinnamon	1	teaspoon lemon juice
1	teaspoon baking powder	1	cup finely chopped walnuts
1	teaspoon ground ginger		Sifted powdered sugar
½	teaspoon salt		Cream Cheese Filling
½	teaspoon ground nutmeg		

1. Allow eggs to stand at room temperature for 30 minutes. Meanwhile, grease a 15×10×1-inch baking pan; line bottom of pan with waxed paper or parchment paper; grease paper and set pan aside. In a small bowl stir together the flour, cinnamon, baking powder, ginger, salt, and nutmeg; set aside.

2. In a large mixing bowl beat eggs with an electric mixer on high speed for 5 minutes. Gradually beat in the granulated sugar. Stir in pumpkin and lemon juice. Fold flour mixture into pumpkin mixture. Spread batter evenly in prepared pan. Top with walnuts.

3. Bake in a 375°F oven for 15 minutes or until top springs back when lightly touched. Immediately loosen edges of cake from pan and turn cake out onto a towel sprinkled with powdered sugar. Remove waxed paper. Roll towel and cake into a spiral starting from one short side of the cake. Cool on a wire rack. Meanwhile, prepare Cream Cheese Filling.

4. Unroll cake; remove towel. Spread cake with Cream Cheese Filling to within 1 inch of edges. Roll up cake. Cover and chill for 2 to 48 hours. Makes 8 servings.

Cream Cheese Filling: In a small bowl beat two 3-ounce packages softened cream cheese, ¼ cup softened butter, and ½ teaspoon vanilla until smooth. Gradually add 1 cup sifted powdered sugar; beat until smooth.

"**A PUMPKIN**-flavored jelly roll wins first prize," exclaimed the editors in the note published with this recipe, which was a prizewinner in our Pumpkin Desserts recipe contest in November 1974. The sumptuous roll-up makes a great way to enjoy the classic autumn flavors of pumpkin and walnuts.

Banana Split Cake

1	cup butter	½	cup milk
4	eggs	1	teaspoon vanilla
3	cups all-purpose flour	½	cup strawberry preserves
2	teaspoons baking powder		Few drops red food coloring
1	teaspoon salt	½	cup presweetened cocoa powder
¼	teaspoon baking soda		(not low calorie)
1½	cups sugar	1	12-ounce jar chocolate fudge ice
½	cup mashed ripe banana (1 large)		cream topping
½	cup dairy sour cream		Vanilla ice cream

BAKING A CAKE in a fluted tube pan must be one of the all-time easiest ways to make dessert look terrific. With this fun recipe, a little strawberry batter and a little chocolate batter marble with a basic banana-cake batter—it's a great potluck choice. Hint: The red food coloring adds a striking color to the strawberry swirl, so don't be tempted to skip it.

1. Allow butter and eggs to stand at room temperature for 30 minutes. Meanwhile, grease and flour a 10-inch fluted tube pan. In a medium bowl stir together the flour, baking powder, salt, and baking soda; set aside.

2. In a large mixing bowl beat butter with an electric mixer on low to medium speed about 30 seconds. Add sugar; beat until fluffy. Add eggs 1 at a time, beating well after each addition. In a small bowl combine banana, sour cream, milk, and vanilla. Alternately add flour mixture and banana mixture to butter mixture, beating on low speed after each addition just until combined.

3. Stir ½ cup strawberry preserves and red food coloring into 1 cup of the batter. Stir cocoa powder into another 1 cup of the batter. Spoon half the remaining plain batter into prepared pan. Spoon strawberry batter over. Top with remaining plain, then chocolate batter.

4. Bake in a 350°F oven for 55 to 65 minutes or until a wooden toothpick inserted near center comes out clean. Cool in pan on a wire rack for 10 minutes; remove from pan. Cool completely on wire rack. In a small saucepan heat ice cream topping until warm. Drizzle over cake. Serve cake with ice cream topped with additional chocolate fudge topping. Makes 12 servings.

70s

Chocolate Chip-Peanut Butter Bread Pudding

sometime during the late '70s and early '80s, dishes "like grandma used to make" snuck back into fashion. One favorite that gained new life during these years is bread pudding, and since then, everyone from superstar chefs to home cooks has come up with innovative adaptations. This one earned honors in a Prize Tested Recipe contest in 1978.

|---|---|
3 cups dry white bread cubes*	2 eggs
½ cup semisweet chocolate pieces	1 teaspoon vanilla
½ cup flaked coconut (optional)	Dash salt
⅔ cup sugar	2 cups milk
½ cup peanut butter	

1. Grease a 2-quart square baking dish; place bread cubes in prepared dish. Sprinkle with chocolate pieces and, if desired, coconut. In a medium mixing bowl beat sugar and peanut butter with an electric mixer on medium speed until well mixed. Beat in eggs, vanilla, and salt. Gradually stir in milk. Pour mixture over bread, pressing down the bread to moisten it all.

2. Bake in a 350°F oven for 40 to 45 minutes or until a knife inserted halfway between the edge and the center comes out clean. Serve warm. Makes 8 servings.

*Note: To dry bread cubes, measure 3½ cups fresh bread cubes. Spread in a single layer in a shallow pan; cover with waxed paper and let stand overnight.

Peppermint Ice Cream Roll

4 eggs	**½** cup granulated sugar
⅓ cup all-purpose flour	Sifted powdered sugar
¼ cup unsweetened cocoa powder	**3** cups peppermint ice cream
¼ teaspoon baking soda	Ganache
½ teaspoon vanilla	Crushed peppermint candy (optional)
⅓ cup granulated sugar	

1. Separate eggs. Allow egg whites and yolks to stand at room temperature for 30 minutes. Lightly grease a 15×10×1-inch baking pan. Line bottom with waxed paper or parchment paper; grease paper and set aside. Sift together the flour, cocoa powder, and baking soda; set aside.

2. In a medium mixing bowl beat egg yolks and vanilla with an electric mixer on high speed for 5 minutes or until thick and lemon colored. Gradually add the ⅓ cup granulated sugar, beating on high speed until sugar is almost dissolved.

3. Thoroughly wash the beaters. In a large mixing bowl beat egg whites with an electric mixer on medium speed until soft peaks form (tips curl). Gradually add the ½ cup granulated sugar, beating until stiff peaks form (tips stand straight). Fold egg yolk mixture into beaten egg whites. Sprinkle flour mixture over egg mixture; fold in gently just until combined. Spread batter evenly in the prepared pan.

4. Bake in a 375°F oven for 12 to 15 minutes or until cake springs back when lightly touched. Immediately loosen edges of cake from pan and turn cake out onto a towel sprinkled with powdered sugar. Remove waxed paper. Roll towel and cake into a spiral starting from a short side of the cake. Cool on a wire rack for 45 to 60 minutes. Meanwhile, prepare Ganache. Unroll cake.

5. In a chilled medium bowl stir ice cream until soft enough to spread. Spread cake with softened ice cream to within 1 inch of edges. Roll up without towel. Spread Ganache over cake roll; place on serving plate. Freeze until set; cover and freeze for 4 hours or overnight. To serve, garnish with crushed candy, if desired. Let stand at room temperature for 10 to 15 minutes before serving. Makes 10 servings.

Ganache: In a small saucepan bring ½ cup whipping cream just to boiling over medium-high heat. Remove from heat. Add 6 ounces chopped semisweet or milk chocolate (do not stir). Let stand 5 minutes. Stir until smooth. Let cool at room temperature for 45 to 60 minutes.

CHOCOLATE AND peppermint marry well in desserts—the peppermint adds refreshment, while the chocolate adds indulgence. Roll them into a pretty cake roll, and you have a hall-of-fame dessert. Another reason we love this dessert is for its make-ahead angle. You'll enjoy your party a lot more knowing this luscious treat is ready and waiting.

Starting from a short side, roll up the warm cake and powdered sugar-coated towel together. Let the cake cool.

THE ALMOND filling in these mini tarts reminded our taste panel of Dutch Letters—those classic pastries oozing with almond paste. This filling covers a touch of raspberry jam, making for a luscious little treat that will be the star of any holiday cookie tray.

Raspberry-Almond Tassies

1	cup all-purpose flour	3	tablespoons butter, softened
¼	teaspoon salt	⅔	cup ground almonds
6	tablespoons butter	¼	teaspoon almond extract
3	to 4 tablespoons cold water	1	slightly beaten egg
4½	teaspoons seedless raspberry jam		Sifted powdered sugar (optional)
½	cup sugar		

1. In a medium bowl stir together the flour and salt. Using a pastry blender, cut in the 6 tablespoons butter until mixture resembles coarse crumbs. Add water, 1 tablespoon at a time, gently tossing mixture with a fork until all the flour mixture is moistened. Form dough into a ball. Wrap in waxed paper. Chill 1 hour.

2. On a floured surface roll pastry to ⅛-inch thickness. Using a 2¾-inch round cookie cutter, cut 18 circles. Fit the circles into 1¾-inch muffin cups. Place ¼ teaspoon jam in each pastry shell. (Do not add more or the jam will burn.)

3. Using an electric mixer, beat together the sugar and the 3 tablespoons butter until creamy. Stir in almonds, almond extract, and egg. Spoon 1 tablespoon of the almond mixture over jam in each pastry shell. Bake in a 400°F oven for 23 to 25 minutes or until golden brown. Remove from pan. Cool on a wire rack. Sift powdered sugar over tops, if desired. Makes 18 tassies.

Here's another one of those great down-home recipes that were especially popular during the "back to the basics" attitudes of the '70s. Hint: If you can't find blackberry jam, substitute red or black raspberry jam.

Oatmeal Jam Bars

1⅓ cups all-purpose flour	2 3-ounce packages cream cheese, softened
¼ teaspoon baking soda	
¼ teaspoon salt	¼ cup butter, softened
¾ cup quick-cooking rolled oats	¾ cup blackberry jam
⅓ cup packed brown sugar	1 teaspoon lemon juice
1 teaspoon finely shredded lemon peel	

1. Grease a 9×9×2-inch baking pan; set aside. In a medium bowl combine the flour, baking soda, and salt. Add oats, brown sugar, and lemon peel; set aside.

2. In a large mixing bowl beat cream cheese and butter with an electric mixer on medium to high speed for 30 seconds. Add the flour mixture and beat on low speed until mixture is crumbly. Set aside 1 cup of the crumb mixture; pat remaining mixture into the bottom of prepared pan. Bake in a 350°F oven for 20 minutes.

3. Meanwhile, in a small bowl stir together jam and lemon juice. Spread over baked crust. Sprinkle with the reserved crumb mixture. Bake for 15 minutes more or until brown. Cool in pan on a wire rack; cut into bars. Makes 36 bars.

Whole Wheat and Fruit Drop Cookies

½ cup butter, softened	¼ teaspoon baking soda
⅓ cup granulated sugar	¼ teaspoon salt
⅓ cup packed brown sugar	¾ cup quick-cooking rolled oats
1 egg	½ cup snipped pitted dates
½ teaspoon vanilla	½ cup raisins
¾ cup whole wheat flour	½ cup chopped walnuts
¼ cup all-purpose flour	½ cup flaked coconut
½ teaspoon baking powder	1½ teaspoons finely shredded orange peel

1. In a large mixing bowl beat butter with an electric mixer on medium to high speed about 30 seconds. Add the granulated sugar and brown sugar; beat until combined, scraping sides of bowl. Beat in the egg and vanilla until combined.

2. In a small bowl stir together the whole wheat flour, all-purpose flour, baking powder, baking soda, and salt. Stir into egg mixture. Stir in oats, dates, raisins, nuts, coconut, and orange peel.

3. Drop dough by teaspoons 2 inches apart onto a lightly greased cookie sheet. Bake in a 375°F oven for 9 to 11 minutes or until edges begin to brown. Cool 1 minute on cookie sheet; remove and cool completely on wire racks. Makes 48 cookies.

THE 1970S saw lots of cooking with natural ingredients, such as whole wheat flour. This recipe is one of the best from that era. When we retested these, we were tempted to rename them "everything-but-the-kitchen-sink cookies" because they roll several favorite baking ingredients into one sweet, nutty, buttery gem.

some like it ...sweet! If you're in that crowd, you'll love this dessert fondue direct from *Snacks and Appetizers* cookbook published in 1974. And if you like the combination of salty and sweet, try pretzels for dipping.

Chocolate-Butter Mint Fondue

1 14-ounce can sweetened condensed milk
1 7-ounce jar marshmallow creme
1 6-ounce package semisweet chocolate pieces (1 cup)
⅓ cup crushed butter mints
¼ cup milk

2 tablespoons crème de cacao (optional)
Strawberries, pineapple chunks, cubed pound cake, shortbread cookies, and/or cream-filled cylinder cookies

1. In a medium saucepan combine the sweetened condensed milk, marshmallow creme, chocolate pieces, and butter mints. Cook and stir over low heat until chocolate melts. Stir in milk and, if desired, crème de cacao. Transfer to fondue pot; place over fondue burner. Dip strawberries, pineapple, pound cake, and/or cookies into fondue mixture, swirling to coat. Makes 6 to 8 servings.

favorites from the 80s

1981

1989

F ast, faster, fastest—that's how cooks wanted their recipes as free time grew more scarce during this decade. And when it came to fat and calories, the question was, how low could we go? Throughout the '80s, our Test Kitchen answered the call—helping people cook faster and healthier. However, comfort, gourmet, and ethnic cooking were hitting their strides too—and we were more than happy to develop plenty of pleasure-filled recipes just for the joy of it. Here are some of our best.

The '80s in our kitchen

1980s: Here's a glimpse inside our Test Kitchen in the 1980s. Then, as now, our seal assured cooks that every recipe had been tested in the *Better Homes and Gardens* Test Kitchen and ensured each recipe is "practical and reliable, and meets our high standard of taste appeal."

1985

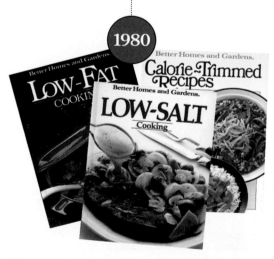

1980

1983

1980s: While "low-cal" was a buzzword in the '60s and '70s, the '80s saw an accelerated interest in the topic of food and nutrition in general, and an even greater focus on slashing calories, fat, and sodium. Throughout the decade, our Test Kitchen pros helped teach cooks to healthfully update their cooking, and the ninth edition of our "red plaid" cookbook, published in 1981, was the first to offer a nutrition analysis with every recipe.

1983: America's love of gourmet cooking, which blossomed in the '60s and '70s, thrived in the '80s as well, and we continued to help cooks caramelize, flambé, deglaze, reduce, and puree their way to fabulous, world-inspired cuisine. And of course, when steps could be made quicker or easier, we were happy to point the way.

1989: Stop and smell the pancakes! While cooks rushed their way through the week's hectic schedule, weekend brunches offered the perfect way to unwind and dine with family and friends.

1986: One of the downsides of working in the middle of the country is that we didn't always have access to the great fish and seafood from America's vast shores—our fish often arrived frozen in blocks. All that changed in the '80s, when purveyors started setting up shop inland, jetting in the catch of the day to the delight of cooks everywhere. Quick-cooking and generally good for you, fish and seafood fit into the decade's call for faster, healthier foods.

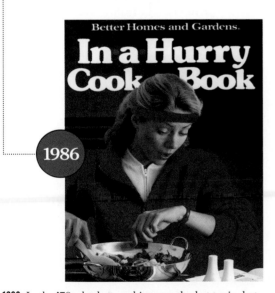

1986: In the '70s, budget cooking was the hot topic, but in the '80s, the issue was minutes, not money. Cooks demanded simpler, quicker recipes, and we obliged, with recipes that required fewer ingredients and less time—while maintaining our high standards. This book promised that "when the race is on, our easy-on-the-cook recipes can make you a winner every time."

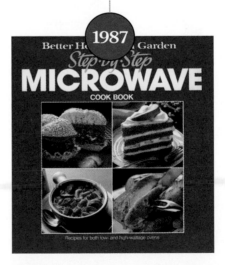

1987: When microwave cooking first came on the scene in the late '70s and early '80s, some consumers were downright wary of them. Our Test Kitchen worked with a major microwave manufacturer to help design the appliance for home cooking; we also helped demystify the microwave for the consumer. This 1987 title is one of our many books that helped time-pressed cooks use the microwave to get food onto the table fast.

80s

These days, the grand and glamorous dinner parties of the past have, for the most part, given way to a new style of casual entertaining. However, for those times when you do want to go a little more elegant, here's one of our favorite stylish sit-down starters from the 1980s.

Cauliflower-Crab Chowder

2 cups loose-pack frozen cauliflower	2 tablespoons chopped pimiento or roasted red sweet pepper
½ cup water	2 tablespoons snipped fresh parsley
3 tablespoons butter	1 tablespoon snipped fresh chives
3 tablespoons all-purpose flour	¼ teaspoon salt
1 14-ounce can vegetable or chicken broth	1 6-ounce package frozen crabmeat, thawed and drained
1¼ cups milk	¼ cup dry white wine or dry sherry
1 3-ounce package cream cheese, cubed	

1. In a medium saucepan combine cauliflower and water. Bring to boiling; reduce heat. Simmer, covered, about 4 minutes or just until crisp-tender. Do not drain. Cut up large pieces of cauliflower; set aside.

2. Meanwhile, in a large saucepan melt butter. Stir in the flour. Add vegetable broth and milk. Cook and stir until slightly thickened and bubbly.

3. Stir in undrained cauliflower, cream cheese, pimiento, parsley, chives, and salt. Stir over low heat until cheese melts. Stir in crab; heat through. Stir in wine. Immediately ladle into soup bowls. Makes 6 appetizer servings.

Brunch Scrambled Eggs

1	10-ounce package frozen chopped spinach, thawed	¼	teaspoon salt
12	eggs	⅛	teaspoon black pepper
½	cup milk	2	tablespoons butter or margarine
½	teaspoon dried oregano or thyme, crushed, or 1½ teaspoons snipped fresh oregano or thyme	1	cup shredded Colby or cheddar cheese (4 ounces)
		1	cup crumbled feta cheese (4 ounces)

1. Drain thawed spinach well, pressing out excess liquid; set aside. In a large bowl beat together eggs, milk, dried oregano (if using), salt, and pepper.

2. In a large skillet melt butter over medium heat; pour in egg mixture. Cook, without stirring, until mixture begins to set on the bottom and around the edges. Using a large spatula, lift and fold partially cooked eggs so uncooked portion flows underneath. Stir in spinach, Colby cheese, and half of the feta cheese. Continue cooking and stirring for 2 to 3 minutes more or until eggs are cooked through and are glossy and moist. Transfer to serving bowl; sprinkle with remaining feta cheese and, if using, the fresh oregano. Makes 6 servings.

While brunch was a fashionable meal in the 1930s, its popularity waned until the 1970s, when an all-out revival occurred. Since then, we've published hundreds of company-special brunch and breakfast recipes. We especially enjoy this one for its bright color, fresh flavors, and its ease.

Cooks in the '80s weren't satisfied with just plain French toast, so many recipes for jazzed-up versions appeared, including this luscious one filled with cream cheese. This recipe is not only one of our favorites, it's been cited as a reader favorite too. Try it for your family's next special breakfast.

Stuffed French Toast

1 **8-ounce package cream cheese, softened**	4 **eggs**
1 **12-ounce jar apricot preserves (about 1 cup)**	1 **cup whipping cream**
1 **teaspoon vanilla**	½ **teaspoon ground nutmeg**
½ **cup chopped walnuts**	½ **teaspoon vanilla**
1 **16-ounce loaf French bread**	½ **cup orange juice**
	Fresh strawberries (optional)

1. In a small mixing bowl beat together cream cheese, 2 tablespoons of the apricot preserves, and the 1 teaspoon vanilla until fluffy. Stir in nuts; set aside. Cut bread into twelve 1¼-inch slices; cut a pocket in the top of each slice. Fill each pocket with about 1½ tablespoons of the cheese mixture.

2. In a medium mixing bowl beat together the eggs, whipping cream, nutmeg, and the ½ teaspoon vanilla. Using tongs, dip the filled bread slices into the egg mixture, being careful not to squeeze out the filling. Cook on a lightly greased griddle over medium heat about 2 minutes on each side or until golden brown. Keep warm in a 300°F oven while cooking the remaining slices.

3. Meanwhile, in a small saucepan heat together the remaining apricot preserves and the orange juice. To serve, drizzle the apricot preserves mixture over hot French toast. If desired, garnish with berries. Makes 10 to 12 slices.

Creamy Ham and Egg Bake

This brunch dish is a top pick of Lori Wilson, who has worked in the *Better Homes and Gardens* Test Kitchen for almost twenty years. She often makes it for birthday parties, baptisms, or other family events. "I can have this prepared the day ahead and just pull it out the next morning and bake——no day-of-party mess!" she says. "They all love how creamy it is, and it is a pretty dish, too, with the colored veggies."

10   eggs
¼   teaspoon salt
2   tablespoons butter or margarine
3   tablespoons butter or margarine
3   tablespoons all-purpose flour
¼   teaspoon black pepper
1¾ cups milk
1½ cups process Gruyère or Swiss cheese, cut up (6 ounces)
2   teaspoons prepared mustard
2   16-ounce packages loose-pack frozen broccoli, corn, and peppers, thawed and well drained
6   ounces fully cooked ham, cut into bite-size strips (about 1 cup)
2   ounces process Gruyère or Swiss cheese, shredded (½ cup)

1. In a medium mixing bowl beat together eggs and salt with a rotary beater. In a 10-inch skillet melt the 2 tablespoons butter over medium heat. Pour in egg mixture. Cook without stirring until mixture begins to set on the bottom and around the edges. Using a large spoon or spatula, lift and fold partially cooked eggs so uncooked portion flows underneath. Continue cooking over medium heat about 4 minutes total or until eggs are cooked throughout but still glossy and moist. Immediately remove eggs from heat; set aside.

2. For sauce, in a 4-quart Dutch oven melt the 3 tablespoons butter. Stir in flour and pepper. Add milk all at once. Cook and stir until thickened and bubbly. Add the 1½ cups cheese and the mustard, stirring until cheese is melted.

3. Stir vegetables and ham into the cheese mixture, then gently fold in eggs. Turn mixture into a 2-quart rectangular baking dish. Cover and chill for 2 to 24 hours.

4. Bake, covered, in a 350°F oven for 45 minutes or until heated through, gently stirring after 15 minutes. Gently stir again after 45 minutes. Sprinkle with the 2 ounces cheese. Bake about 5 minutes more or until cheese is melted. Makes 12 servings.

Coq au Vin Rosettes

8 medium skinless, boneless chicken
   breast halves
2 tablespoons butter or margarine
3 cups sliced fresh mushrooms
   (8-ounces)
½ cup chopped onion
¾ cup dry white wine
½ teaspoon dried tarragon, crushed
½ teaspoon white pepper
⅛ teaspoon salt
8 lasagna noodles

1 8-ounce package cream cheese,
   cut up
½ cup dairy sour cream
2 tablespoons all-purpose flour
½ cup half-and-half, light cream, or milk
1 cup shredded Gruyère cheese
   (4 ounces)
1 cup shredded Muenster cheese
   (4 ounces)
   Slivered almonds, toasted (optional)

1. Cut chicken into 1-inch pieces. In a skillet melt butter over medium-high heat. Add mushrooms and onion; cook for 4 to 5 minutes or until tender, stirring occasionally. Add chicken, wine, tarragon, white pepper, and salt. Bring just to boiling; reduce heat. Simmer, covered, for 5 minutes, stirring once. Remove from heat.

2. Meanwhile, cook lasagna noodles according to package directions. Halve each noodle lengthwise. Curl each noodle half into a 2½ inch-diameter ring; place noodle rings, cut sides down, in a 3-quart rectangular baking dish. Using a slotted spoon, spoon chicken mixture into center of noodle rings, reserving the liquid in skillet. Add the cream cheese to reserved liquid; heat and stir just until cream cheese is melted.

3. In a small bowl stir together sour cream and flour; stir in half-and-half. Add the sour cream mixture and cheeses to the cream cheese mixture in skillet. Cook and stir over medium heat until thickened and bubbly.

4. Spoon cheese mixture over filled rings in baking dish. If desired, sprinkle with slivered almonds. Bake, covered, in a 325°F oven for 35 minutes or until heated through. Makes 8 servings.

As if all the great flavors of coq au vin weren't enough, this recipe rolls them up in a pasta "rosette" (it's simply a lasagne noodle, halved lengthwise), then tops them with an opulent cream sauce. The recipe hails from our prizewinning recipes files. It's a great dinner party dish because you can prepare it just before guests arrive, then slide it in the oven after you welcome them.

One of our first chicken fricassee dishes was an easy oven meal made with canned soup in the frugal, energy-rationing war years of the 1940s. With its fresh and sprightly tarragon-lemon flavors and luscious cream sauce, this '80s update reflects that decade's love of all things gourmet.

· · · ·   IF YOU ARE WHAT YOU EAT, START

CLUCKING

Chicken seems to hit the spot these days. On average, you'll each down about 60 pounds of the bird this year—that's about 20 chickens all to yourself. Compare that to 40 pounds each 10 years ago.

No doubt your heightened awareness of the low-cholesterol and low-calorie benefits of eating chicken accounts for some of the increase in its popularity, but evidence shows that convenience, too, is important. Boneless chicken pieces that pop right into a frying pan or microwave oven or onto the grill are selling better than ever these days.

Lemon-Tarragon Chicken Fricassee

¼ cup all-purpose flour	1 teaspoon dried tarragon, crushed
½ teaspoon salt	½ teaspoon finely shredded lemon peel
¼ teaspoon black pepper	¼ teaspoon black pepper
2½ to 3 pounds meaty chicken pieces (breast halves, thighs, and drumsticks)	1 bay leaf
	1 cup carrots, cut in matchstick strips
2 tablespoons cooking oil or shortening	1 tablespoon butter or margarine
3 stalks celery, bias-sliced (1½ cups)	1 tablespoon all-purpose flour
1 large onion, chopped (1 cup)	⅔ cup milk
1 cup water	2 egg yolks
2 teaspoons instant chicken bouillon granules	¼ cup snipped fresh parsley
	2 tablespoons lemon juice

1. Combine the ¼ cup flour, the salt, and ¼ teaspoon pepper in a large plastic bag. Add chicken pieces, one or two at a time; seal and shake to coat with flour mixture. In a 12-inch skillet cook chicken in hot oil, uncovered, over medium heat about 15 minutes or until light brown, turning to brown evenly. Remove chicken; drain off all but 2 tablespoons fat.

2. Add celery and onion to skillet. Cook and stir 2 minutes. Carefully add water, bouillon granules, tarragon, lemon peel, ¼ teaspoon pepper, and bay leaf. Bring to boiling, scraping up browned bits. Add chicken and carrot; reduce heat. Simmer, covered, for 35 to 40 minutes or until chicken is tender and no longer pink.

3. Transfer chicken to a warm platter; cover to keep warm. Discard bay leaf. Remove vegetables with slotted spoon; set aside. For sauce, skim fat from pan juices. Measure and reserve ¾ cup juices. In the same skillet melt butter. Stir in the 1 tablespoon flour. Add reserved juices and milk all at once. Cook and stir until thickened and bubbly; cook and stir 1 minute more.

4. In a small bowl beat egg yolks. Gradually stir in thickened milk mixture. Return all to skillet. Cook and stir 1 minute. Stir in vegetables, parsley, and lemon juice; heat through. Spoon sauce and vegetables over chicken. Makes 6 servings.

Beef and Noodles

1 pound boneless beef round steak or chuck roast	3 cups beef broth
¼ cup all-purpose flour	1 teaspoon dried marjoram or basil, crushed
1 tablespoon cooking oil	¼ teaspoon black pepper
½ cup chopped onion (1 medium)	8 ounces frozen noodles
2 cloves garlic, minced	2 tablespoons snipped fresh parsley

1. Trim fat from meat. Cut meat into ¾-inch cubes. Coat meat with the flour. In a large saucepan brown half of the coated meat in hot oil. Remove from saucepan. Brown the remaining meat with the onion and garlic, adding more oil, if necessary. Drain off fat. Return all meat to the saucepan.

2. Stir in the broth, marjoram, and pepper. Bring to boiling; reduce heat. Simmer, covered, for 1¼ to 1½ hours or until meat is tender.

3. Stir noodles into broth mixture. Bring to boiling; reduce heat. Cook, uncovered, for 25 to 30 minutes or until noodles are tender. Sprinkle with parsley. Makes 4 servings.

In general, pasta dishes aren't served with potatoes. For some people, however, the only way to serve this homey dish is over a big scoop of mashed potatoes. In fact, it's one of the staightest paths to comfort food heaven we know!

Here's another dinner-party dish from the gourmet-food-loving 1980s. The hearty, warming stew, with its tender chunks of veal, mushrooms, and leeks, makes perfect winter fare. Then as now, guests love getting their own pastry-topped pie in an individual au gratin dish.

Veal Stew with Pastry Topper

2	pounds boneless veal		1	cup dry white wine
½	cup all-purpose flour		3	cloves garlic, minced
½	teaspoon salt		¾	teaspoon dried thyme, crushed
¼	teaspoon black pepper		½	teaspoon dried rosemary, crushed
2	tablespoons cooking oil		½	teaspoon finely shredded lemon peel
4	cups mushrooms, quartered		2	egg yolks, slightly beaten
6	medium leeks, thinly sliced (2 cups)		½	cup whipping cream
3	medium carrots, bias-sliced ½ inch (1¼ cups)			Rich Pastry
1	14-ounce can chicken broth		1	beaten egg
				Salt and black pepper (optional)

1. Cut meat into ¾-inch cubes. In a plastic bag combine the flour, the ½ teaspoon salt, and the ¼ teaspoon pepper. Add meat cubes to flour mixture, a few at a time, shaking to coat. In a Dutch oven brown meat, half at a time, in hot oil. Add more oil, if necessary, to brown second half of meat. Return all meat to Dutch oven. Stir in the mushrooms, leeks, carrots, broth, wine, garlic, thyme, rosemary, and lemon peel. Bring to boiling; reduce heat. Simmer, covered, for 20 to 30 minutes or until meat is tender, stirring occasionally.

2. Beat together egg yolks and cream. Stir about 1 cup of the hot meat mixture into egg yolk mixture. Stir egg yolk mixture into meat mixture in Dutch oven, stirring to combine. Remove meat mixture from heat.

3. Meanwhile, prepare, roll out, and cut Rich Pastry. Divide meat mixture among six 10- or 12-ounce au gratin dishes or single-serving baking dishes. Make decorative slits or cutouts in pastry for steam to escape. Place pastry over each casserole. Fold under extra pastry and flute to edge of dish. Brush pastry with beaten egg. Layer on cutouts made from pastry scraps and brush with egg. Transfer dishes to baking sheets. Bake in a 450°F oven for 20 to 25 minutes or until pastry is golden. Season to taste with additional salt and pepper, if desired. Makes 6 servings.

Rich Pastry: In a bowl combine 2 cups all-purpose flour and ½ teaspoon salt. Cut in ½ cup shortening and ¼ cup cold butter until mixture resembles coarse crumbs. Make a well in the center. Beat together 1 egg yolk and ¼ cup cold water; add to flour mixture. Using a fork, stir until dough forms a ball. Divide dough in half. Wrap each ball in plastic wrap; freeze for 20 minutes. On a lightly floured surface roll each half into a rectangle about ⅛ to ¼ inch thick; from each half, cut 3 rounds or ovals measuring 1 inch larger than the au gratin dishes. Use small cutters to make cutouts from pastry scraps.

In the '70s and early '80s, as more men became more interested in cooking, *Better Homes and Gardens* magazine ran a monthly feature entitled "He Cooks," with recipes sent in from men all over the country. About his recipe, the bachelor cook who concocted these said, "My guests love the filets, and they're a great way to dress up ground beef." These days, the topic of men in the kitchen doesn't merit special mention. However, reluctant cooks might find this recipe worthy of some time at the grill.

Poor Boy Filets

10 slices bacon	3 tablespoons finely chopped pimiento-stuffed olives
1 pound lean ground beef	
1/8 teaspoon salt	2 tablespoons finely chopped onion
1/4 teaspoon lemon-pepper seasoning	2 tablespoons finely chopped green sweet pepper
1/4 cup grated Parmesan cheese	
1 4-ounce can mushroom stems and pieces, drained and chopped	Halved cherry tomatoes (optional)

1. In a very large skillet partially cook bacon just until lightly browned, but still soft. Drain on paper towels. Set aside.

2. Pat ground beef on waxed paper into a 12×7½-inch rectangle that is ¼ inch thick. Sprinkle lightly with salt and lemon pepper; top with cheese. Combine mushrooms, olives, onion, and sweet pepper; sprinkle evenly over meat; lightly press into meat.

3. Carefully roll meat into a spiral, starting from a short side. Cut into 1½-inch slices. Wrap the edge of each slice with two strips of partially cooked bacon, overlapping as needed and securing ends with wooden picks.

4. Grill meat on the rack of an uncovered grill directly over medium coals for 10 minutes. Turn meat over and grill 10 minutes more or until meat is done (160°F). To serve, transfer to a platter and garnish with cherry tomatoes, if desired. Makes 5 servings.

Moussaka

2	1-pound eggplants, peeled and cut into ½-inch slices
¼	cup cooking oil
2	pounds ground lamb or ground beef
1	cup chopped onion (1 large)
1	clove garlic, minced
1	8-ounce can tomato sauce
¾	cup dry red wine
2	tablespoons snipped fresh parsley
¾	teaspoon salt
¼	teaspoon dried oregano, crushed
¼	teaspoon ground cinnamon
1	beaten egg
¼	cup butter or margarine
¼	cup all-purpose flour
½	teaspoon salt
	Dash black pepper
2	cups milk
3	eggs
½	cup grated Parmesan cheese
	Ground cinnamon
	Snipped fresh parsley (optional)

1. Brush both sides of eggplant slices with the oil. In a large skillet brown eggplant slices over medium heat about 2 minutes per side. Drain; set aside.

2. In the same skillet cook ground lamb, half at a time, until meat is brown, cooking the onion and garlic with the second half of meat. Drain off fat. Return all meat to skillet. Stir in the tomato sauce, wine, the 2 tablespoons parsley, the ¾ teaspoon salt, oregano, and the ¼ teaspoon cinnamon. Heat to boiling; reduce heat. Simmer, uncovered, for 10 minutes or until most of the liquid is absorbed. Cool mixture slightly. Stir ½ cup of the meat mixture into the 1 beaten egg. Stir egg mixture into meat mixture in skillet.

3. Meanwhile, in a medium saucepan melt the butter. Stir in the flour, the ½ teaspoon salt, and pepper. Add milk all at once. Cook and stir until thickened and bubbly. Cook and stir for 1 minute more. In a medium bowl beat the 3 eggs. Gradually stir the thickened milk mixture into the beaten eggs.

4. In a 3-quart rectangular baking dish arrange half of the eggplant slices. Spread the meat mixture over the eggplant slices; top with remaining eggplant slices. Pour the hot egg mixture over all. Top with Parmesan cheese and sprinkle lightly with additional cinnamon. Bake, uncovered, in a 325°F oven for 35 to 40 minutes or until edges are bubbly. Let stand 10 minutes before serving. Cut into squares to serve. Sprinkle with additional parsley, if desired. Makes 8 to 10 servings.

This layered lamb-eggplant dish has been a classic of Greek cuisine for a long time, but it took the adventursome '80s to make Moussaka mainstream! One of the reasons this still ranks as a favorite is its crowd-pleasing party appeal. Put it together, pop it in the oven, and let the fun begin.

A favorite from the pages of our 1981 "red plaid" cookbook, this crowd-pleasing recipe may be one of our most famous potluck favorites. Take it along to your next summertime bring-a-dish gathering—everyone will be glad you did.

Baked Bean Quintet

1 cup chopped onion (1 large)	1 15-ounce can garbanzo beans, rinsed and drained
6 slices bacon, cut up	¾ cup catsup
1 clove garlic, minced	½ cup molasses
1 16-ounce can lima beans, rinsed and drained	¼ cup packed brown sugar
1 16-ounce can pork and beans in tomato sauce	1 tablespoon prepared mustard
1 15½-ounce can red kidney beans, rinsed and drained	1 tablespoon Worcestershire sauce
1 15-ounce can butter beans, rinsed and drained	Cooked bacon (optional)

1. In a skillet cook the onion, bacon, and garlic until bacon is crisp and onion is tender; drain. In a bowl combine onion mixture, lima beans, pork and beans, kidney beans, butter beans, garbanzo beans, catsup, molasses, brown sugar, mustard, and Worcestershire sauce. Transfer bean mixture to a 3-quart casserole. Bake, covered, in a 375°F oven for 1 hour. If desired, top with additional cooked bacon. Makes 12 to 16 servings.

Slow-cooker directions: Prepare bean mixture as above. Transfer to a 3½- or 4-quart electric slow cooker. Cover and cook on low-heat setting for 10 to 12 hours or on high-heat setting for 4 to 5 hours.

Praline Yam Casserole

6 medium yams or sweet potatoes (2 pounds)	1 teaspoon vanilla
⅓ cup milk	½ teaspoon salt
¼ cup packed brown sugar	3 tablespoons butter or margarine
2 tablespoons butter or margarine, melted	⅓ cup packed brown sugar
1 egg	3 tablespoons all-purpose flour
	⅓ cup chopped pecans

1. Scrub yams or sweet potatoes. Cut off woody portions and ends.

2. In a 4-quart Dutch oven cook yams, covered, in enough boiling salted water to cover for 25 to 30 minutes or until tender. Drain and cool slightly. Peel and cut up yams.

3. Mash yams with a potato masher or beat with an electric mixer on low speed. Add milk, the ¼ cup brown sugar, the 2 tablespoons melted butter, the egg, vanilla, and salt. Beat until fluffy. Add additional milk, if desired. Turn into a greased 1½-quart casserole or baking dish.

4. In a small saucepan melt 3 tablespoons butter over low heat. Stir in ⅓ cup brown sugar, flour, and pecans. Mix well. Spoon pecan mixture over yam mixture. Bake, uncovered, in a 350°F oven for 35 minutes or until heated through. Makes 8 servings.

Cajun cooking was all the rage in the mid-1980s. This yummy yam dish, inspired by the famous pralines of New Orleans, comes straight from the pages of the *Cajun Cookbook*, published in 1987. It's sweet, rich, and buttery—a spoonful goes a long way—so it's a great choice to tote to a holiday potluck gathering.

Spanish Rice

6	slices bacon	1	tablespoon packed brown sugar
1	medium onion, finely chopped (½ cup)	1	tablespoon Worcestershire sauce
1	small green sweet pepper, finely chopped (½ cup)	1	teaspoon salt
1	28-ounce can diced tomatoes	1	teaspoon chili powder
1	cup water	⅛	teaspoon black pepper
¾	cup long grain rice		Dash bottled hot pepper sauce
			Shredded cheddar cheese (optional)

1. In a 10-inch skillet cook bacon until crisp. Drain on paper towels, reserving 2 tablespoons of drippings in skillet; crumble bacon and set aside. In the reserved drippings cook onion and sweet pepper over medium heat until tender. Stir in undrained tomatoes, water, rice, brown sugar, Worcestershire sauce, salt, chili powder, black pepper, and hot pepper sauce. Simmer, covered, about 30 minutes or until rice is tender and most of the liquid is absorbed. Top with the crumbled bacon. Sprinkle with shredded cheddar cheese, if desired. Makes 6 servings.

Like many Test Kitchen home economists and food editors, Juliana Hale grew up cooking from our famous "red plaid" cookbook long before she ever dreamed of joining the Test Kitchen staff. She remembers making this recipe as a teenager in the 1980s, and she still claims it's our best-ever version of Spanish Rice. "Prep time is quick," she says, "plus it's just loaded with flavor, including a nice smokiness from the bacon."

We've featured a lot of coffee cakes over the past 75 years, but this rich, moist beauty from 1987 creates a stir wherever it's served. Remember it when it's your turn to bring treats to the office—"hands-on" time is just a quick 15 minutes before you pop it in the oven. That's hardly any longer than it takes to stop at the store for donuts—and this is so much better!

Cream Cheese and Raspberry Coffee Cake

1 8-ounce package cream cheese or reduced-fat cream cheese (Neufchâtel), softened	¼ cup milk
	½ teaspoon vanilla
	1 teaspoon baking powder
1 cup granulated sugar	½ teaspoon baking soda
½ cup butter, softened	¼ teaspoon salt
1¾ cups all-purpose flour	½ cup seedless raspberry preserves
2 eggs	Sifted powdered sugar

1. Grease and flour a 13×9×2-inch baking pan; set aside. In a large mixing bowl beat cream cheese, granulated sugar, and butter with an electric mixer on medium speed until combined. Add half of the flour, the eggs, milk, vanilla, baking powder, baking soda, and salt. Beat about 2 minutes or until well combined. Beat in remaining flour on low speed just until combined. Spread batter evenly in prepared baking pan. Spoon preserves in 8 to 10 portions on top of batter. With a knife, swirl preserves into batter to marble.

2. Bake in a 350°F oven for 30 to 35 minutes or until a wooden toothpick inserted near center comes out clean. Cool slightly in pan on a wire rack. Sift powdered sugar over top. Cut into squares; serve warm. Makes 24 servings.

Overnight Three-Grain Waffles

1¼	cups all-purpose flour		½	teaspoon salt
1	cup yellow cornmeal		2	cups milk
½	cup oat bran		2	eggs
3	tablespoons sugar		⅓	cup cooking oil
1	package active dry yeast			Praline Sauce or maple syrup

1. In large mixing bowl combine the flour, cornmeal, bran, sugar, yeast, and salt. Add the milk, eggs, and oil; beat with a rotary beater or an electric mixer for 1 minute on medium speed until thoroughly combined. Cover loosely and let stand for 1 hour at room temperature or for 2 to 24 hours in the refrigerator until mixture is bubbly and slightly thickened.

2. Meanwhile, prepare Praline Sauce. Stir batter. Pour batter into a preheated, lightly greased waffle baker. (Check manufacturer's directions for amount of batter to use.) Close lid quickly; do not open during baking. Bake accordingly to manufacturer's directions. Use a fork to remove the baked waffle from the grid. Keep hot. Repeat with remaining batter. Serve immediately with Praline Sauce. Makes 6 (4-inch) waffles.

Praline Sauce: In a small saucepan combine ¾ cup granulated sugar, ¾ cup packed brown sugar, and ½ cup half-and-half or light cream. Cook and stir over medium-high heat until boiling, stirring constantly to dissolve sugars. Boil, uncovered, for 1 minute. Remove from heat. Stir in ⅓ cup coarsely chopped pecans, 1 tablespoon butter or margarine, and ½ teaspoon vanilla. Stir until butter melts. Makes 1½ cups sauce.

"This tastes like something you'd get at a fancy bed and breakfast," said one Test Kitchen pro at a taste panel. So, if you want to treat family or overnight guests to a gracious breakfast, whip up a batch of these light and fluffy waffles. P.S. They're a favorite of former Test Kitchen Director Sharon Stilwell, a 29-year veteran of the kitchen who knows a thing or two about waffles.

"**Believe it** or not, this irresistible cake is as easy as making brownies," reads the taste panel's note attached to this 1981 recipe. "First, you mix and bake the easy one-bowl fudgy cake layer. Second, decorate it with a whipped cream lattice. Third, add canned strawberry and apricot pie fillings, sliced almonds, and broken milk chocolate bars." Test Kitchen pro Maryellyn Krantz says she still makes this easy recipe when she needs a special, impressive dessert.

Candy Bar Cake

½ cup butter
3 tablespoons unsweetened cocoa
   powder
1 cup all-purpose flour
1 cup sugar
½ teaspoon baking soda
¼ teaspoon salt
1 slightly beaten egg
¼ cup buttermilk or sour milk*

1 teaspoon vanilla
1 cup whipping cream
3 tablespoons sugar
1 21-ounce can strawberry pie filling
1 21-ounce can apricot pie filling
   Sliced almonds
5 bars (1.5 ounces each) plain milk
   chocolate

1. Grease and lightly flour one 8×1½-inch round baking pan; set aside. In a small saucepan combine butter, ¼ cup water, and unsweetened cocoa powder. Bring to boiling, stirring constantly. Remove from heat. In a medium bowl stir together the flour, the 1 cup sugar, the baking soda, and salt; stir in egg, buttermilk, and vanilla. Blend in cocoa mixture. Pour into prepared pan. Bake in a 350°F oven for 40 to 45 minutes or until a toothpick inserted near the center comes out clean. Cool for 10 minutes on a wire rack. Remove from pan; cool completely on wire rack.

2. To assemble cake, beat whipping cream and the 3 tablespoons sugar until stiff peaks form (tips stand straight). On a serving plate frost top and sides of cake with a thin layer of the whipped cream. Using a decorator tube and tip, pipe remaining whipped cream over top of cake in a lattice design, finishing with a border around the top edge. Spoon some strawberry filling into every other diamond in lattice. Spoon some apricot filling into remaining lattice diamonds. (Chill remaining pie filling for another use.) Sprinkle almonds on cake. Break chocolate bars crosswise into fourths, making 20 pieces total. Arrange, smooth side out and edges overlapping, around side of cake. Press into cream to secure. Chill until serving time or up to 2 hours. To cut cake, remove chocolate pieces. Makes 10 servings.

*To make sour milk: For 1 cup sour milk, place 1 tablespoon lemon juice or vinegar in a glass measuring cup. Add enough milk to make 1 cup total liquid; stir. Let mixture stand for 5 minutes before using.

June 1981 · $1.25

Better Homes

and Gardens®

Decorating: Furniture arrangements that make the most of space

Gardening: Get instant flowers with bedding plants

Food: Easy-does-it summer parties with pointers from the pros

Survey: How is work affecting American families?

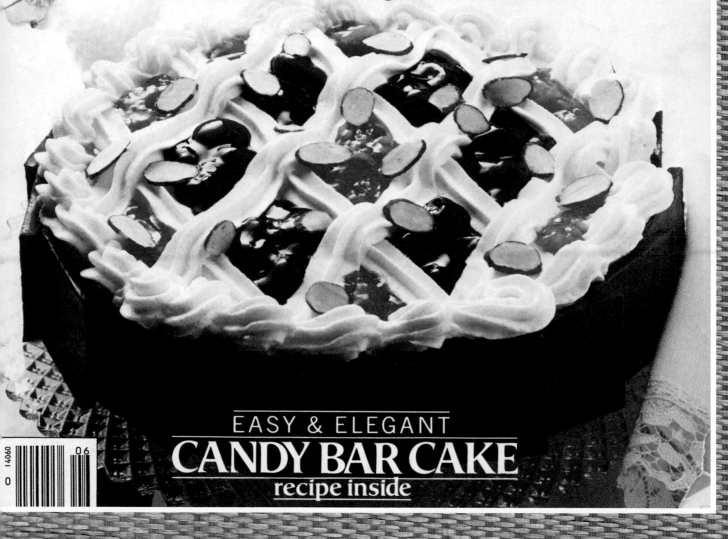

EASY & ELEGANT
CANDY BAR CAKE
recipe inside

Butter Pecan Ice Cream

1 cup coarsely chopped pecans	2 cups packed brown sugar
½ cup granulated sugar	1 tablespoon vanilla
2 tablespoons butter	4 cups whipping cream
4 cups half-and-half or light cream	

1. In a heavy 8-inch skillet combine pecans, granulated sugar, and butter. Cook mixture over medium heat, stirring constantly with a wooden spoon, for 6 to 8 minutes or until sugar melts and turns a rich brown color.

2. Remove from heat and spread nuts on a buttered baking sheet or foil; separate into clusters and cool. Break clusters into small chunks.

3. In a large bowl combine half-and-half, brown sugar, and vanilla; stir until sugar is dissolved. Stir in the whipping cream. Freeze cream mixture in a 4- to 5-quart ice cream freezer according to the manufacturer's directions. Stir in pecan mixture.* Ripen 4 hours. Makes 16 servings (2 quarts).

*Note: Stirring the pecan mixture into the thickened ice cream mixture just before ripening prevents the nuts from wrapping around the paddle.

Our taste panel's response to this refound treasure was unanimous—you just can't buy ice cream like this, not even with today's gourmet brands. Candied pecans provide this version's taste treat. Yum!

80s

In September 1988,

this luscious frozen dessert took top honors in the Favorite Ice Creams Prize Tested Recipe contest. "So rich and creamy—it's just like eating cheesecake!" exclaimed the note with the recipe at the time. Remember this when you want a cool, refreshing—but incredibly satisfying—summer dessert.

Cream Cheese Ice Cream

5 cups half-and-half or light cream
2½ cups sugar
4 beaten eggs
3 8-ounce packages cream cheese or reduced-fat cream cheese (Neufchâtel), softened

1 teaspoon finely shredded lemon peel
2 tablespoons lemon juice
2 teaspoons vanilla
Fresh blueberries, nectarines, and/or dark cherries (optional)

1. In a large saucepan combine 3 cups of the half-and-half, the sugar, and eggs. Cook and stir over medium heat just until boiling. In a large mixing bowl beat cream cheese with an electric mixer until smooth; gradually beat in hot mixture. Cover; chill thoroughly.

2. Stir in the remaining half-and-half, lemon peel, lemon juice, and vanilla. Freeze in a 4- or 5-quart ice cream freezer according to the manufacturer's directions. Ripen for 4 hours. Garnish each serving with a choice of fresh fruit, if desired. Makes 24 servings (3 quarts).

Chocolate-Cherry Cookies

1½ cups all-purpose flour
½ cup unsweetened cocoa powder
½ cup butter, softened
1 cup sugar
¼ teaspoon baking soda
¼ teaspoon baking powder
¼ teaspoon salt

1 egg
1½ teaspoons vanilla
48 maraschino cherries* (about one 10-ounce jar), undrained
1 6-ounce package semisweet chocolate pieces (1 cup)
½ cup sweetened condensed milk

1. In a small bowl combine the flour and cocoa powder; set aside. In a large mixing bowl beat butter with an electric mixer on medium to high speed for 30 seconds. Add the sugar, baking soda, baking powder, and salt; beat until combined. Beat in the egg and vanilla. Gradually beat in flour mixture.

2. Shape dough into 1-inch balls. Place about 2 inches apart on an ungreased cookie sheet. Press down center of each ball with your thumb. Drain maraschino cherries, reserving juice. Place a cherry in the center of each cookie.

3. For frosting, in a small saucepan combine the chocolate pieces and sweetened condensed milk; heat until chocolate is melted. Stir in 4 teaspoons reserved cherry juice.

4. Spoon about 1 teaspoon frosting over each cherry, spreading to cover cherry. (If necessary, thin frosting with additional cherry juice.) Bake in a 350°F oven about 10 minutes or until edges are firm. Cool on cookie sheet for 1 minute. Transfer to wire racks to cool. Makes 48 cookies.

*Note: If cherries are large, halve them before using.

To store: Place cookies in layers separated by waxed paper in an airtight container; cover. Store at room temperature for up to 3 days or freeze for up to 3 months.

Test Kitchen technical assistant Barb Allen, who fields most calls to the kitchen, says that readers still often request this recipe, even though it was published more than 20 years ago. We love it too—for many reasons: The cookies are easily frosted before they're baked, each has a buried cherry surprise, and of course, the rich, fudgy flavor is irresistible.

Giant Ginger Cookies

Chewy and delicious, these cookies are giants in both size and snappy ginger flavor. They're an all-time favorite of Test Kitchen pro Colleen Weeden, who makes them for her family every Christmas, and one of those recipes that readers call in to request again and again. These cookies prove that sometimes the simplest treats are the best loved. Hint: For chewier cookies, make them with shortening instead of butter.

2¼	cups all-purpose flour	¾	cup butter or shortening
2	teaspoons ground ginger	1	cup sugar
1	teaspoon baking soda	1	egg
¾	teaspoon ground cinnamon	¼	cup molasses
½	teaspoon ground cloves	2	tablespoons coarse or regular sugar
⅛	teaspoon salt		

1. In a medium bowl combine the flour, ginger, baking soda, cinnamon, cloves, and salt; set aside.

2. In a large mixing bowl beat butter with an electric mixer on low speed for 30 seconds. Gradually add the 1 cup sugar; beat until fluffy. Add the egg and molasses; beat well. Stir the flour mixture into the egg mixture.

3. Shape dough into 1½-inch balls (1 heaping tablespoon dough each). Roll balls in the 2 tablespoons sugar and place on ungreased cookie sheets about 2½ inches apart.

4. Bake in a 350°F oven about 10 minutes or until light brown but still puffed. (Do not overbake.) Let stand on cookie sheets for 2 minutes; transfer to a wire rack and let cool. Makes about 24 cookies.

Oatmeal-Caramel Bars

1½ **cups quick-cooking rolled oats**
¾ **cup all-purpose flour**
⅔ **cup packed brown sugar**
¼ **teaspoon baking soda**
⅔ **cup butter, melted**
25 **vanilla caramels**

2 **tablespoons butter**
1 **tablespoon milk**
½ **cup chopped nuts**
⅓ **cup miniature semisweet chocolate**
    pieces

1. In a bowl stir together the oats, flour, brown sugar, and baking soda. Add the melted butter; stir until well combined. Set aside 1 cup of the oat mixture for topping.

2. Pat the remaining oat mixture into a foil-lined 8×8×2-inch baking pan. Bake in a 350°F oven for 10 minutes.

3. Meanwhile, for filling, in a small heavy saucepan combine caramels, the 2 tablespoons butter, and milk. Cook and stir over low heat just until melted.

4. Carefully spread filling on baked crust. Sprinkle with nuts, chocolate pieces, and remaining oat mixture. Bake in the 350°F oven about 20 minutes more or until top is golden. Cool in pan on a wire rack. Using the foil, lift out of the pan. Cut into bars. Makes 24 bars.

Exquisite Almond Truffles

16 ounces white chocolate baking pieces	18 ounces semisweet chocolate pieces (3 cups)
¼ cup whipping cream	3 tablespoons shortening
¼ cup cream of coconut	4 ounces white chocolate baking pieces
1 cup sliced almonds, toasted and chopped	2 tablespoons shortening
2 tablespoons amaretto	

1. For filling, in a medium saucepan heat and stir the 16 ounces white chocolate, the whipping cream, and cream of coconut just until the white chocolate is melted. Remove from heat. Stir in chopped almonds and amaretto. Cover; freeze for 2 hours or until firm. Divide filling into 48 portions; shape each portion into a ball. Freeze for 15 minutes.

2. Meanwhile, in a 4-cup glass measure combine the semisweet chocolate pieces and the 3 tablespoons shortening. In a large glass bowl pour very warm tap water (100°F to 110°F) to a depth of 1 inch. Place the glass measure with semisweet chocolate mixture inside the large bowl of water. (Water should cover bottom half of the glass measure.) Stir semisweet chocolate mixture constantly with a rubber spatula until chocolate is completely melted and smooth. This step takes about 20 minutes; don't rush it. If water cools, remove glass measure. Discard cool water; add warm water. Return glass measure to bowl with water.

3. Using a fork, dip frozen balls of filling, one at a time, into melted chocolate mixture; place on a baking sheet lined with waxed paper. Freeze for 15 minutes.

4. Meanwhile, in a 1-cup glass measure combine the 4 ounces white chocolate and the 2 tablespoons shortening; melt in a bowl of very warm water as directed above. Drizzle over truffles. Chill for a few minutes until set. Makes 48 truffles.

As tastes became more sophisticated in the 1980s, chocolate lovers got turned on to truffles—those rich, creamy, chocolate confections imbued with a variety of flavors. It wasn't long before we perfected a way to make these gourmet delights at home. Hint: If you like, instead of the melted semisweet chocolate, dip the truffles in melted white chocolate baking pieces and dust them in cocoa powder. Or skip the white chocolate drizzle and roll them in chopped toasted pecans. No matter which garnish you choose, they're easy to love.

favorites from the
90s
and today

2002

2002

I t's an exciting time to work in the *Better Homes and Gardens* Test Kitchen. Never has there been a better supply of fresh, quality foods—from herbs sown by local growers to artisinal cheeses from afar—more readily available to home cooks; never has there been more interest in global cuisine, in all its wondrous diversity. Perhaps best of all, people everyhere are heading back to the family table, rediscovering the simple but essential joys to be found there. And we're having the times of our lives pointing the way.

The '90s in our kitchen

2000: The new millennium brought a new approach to healthful eating. Out with restrictive diets and obsessing about fat and calories, in with moderation, common sense, and loving what you eat. *Smart Diet* is just one of the many books we've worked on throughout the last decade that takes a realistic and pleasure-filled approach to eating well.

2000

1990s: While we've most always preferred fresh herbs over dried in cooking, it wasn't until the '90s that they were available nationwide to the home cook. These days, we can't get enough of them because few ingredients add so much flavor and freshness with so little effort. We also enjoy using herbs in unexpected ways to add flavor to everything from scones to sorbet.

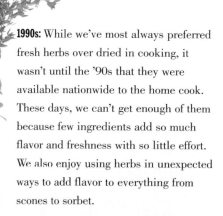

1990s

1998

1998: Fresh and simple—that's today's angle to fast cooking, and the premise is this: In general, the less you mess with the market-fresh, high-quality ingredients readily available today, the better they taste. Debuting in 1998, the groundbreaking *Better Homes and Gardens Fresh and Simple* series showed cooks how to simply combine flavor-packed ingredients to make fantastic, fuss-free fare.

Today

Today: Although fast-paced lifestyles threaten to nibble away at family mealtime, there's a movement afoot in homes everywhere to dine in more often. And as long as there are cooks who want to get a meal on the table, our Test Kitchen will be here to show them how.

Dinner *from the* Heart

There was a time, long before the days of fast-forward lifestyles, when families sat down together at the dinner table. One generation nutured the next on a diet of comfort and support as well as tasty victuals.

by Carrie Holcomb and Joy Taylor

Today

Today: To the mid-20th-century cook, convenience most often came from a can. Today, salsa, pesto, refrigerated pasta and polenta, packaged salads, pizza shells, chutney, curry paste, and a world of other terrific, easy-to-use ingredients are redefining "jiffy cooking." We love calling on these intriguing products to help cooks bring lively, full-flavored meals to the table in less time than ever.

Today

Today: In decades past, much international cooking focused on the cuisine of Europe. Today we're casting our net even farther for inspiration. We're developing recipes that call on an array of global ingredients, techniques, and ideas to help cooks bring a new world of bold, rich flavors to their tables.

Today

BETTER HOMES AND GARDENS TEST KITCHEN ®

Today: Here's a peak inside the Test Kitchen today. At right, our seal continues to ensure that each recipe is "practical and reliable, and meets our high standards of taste appeal."

90s

Sometime in the '90s, cocktails crept back into style, and these sweet, hot, and crunchy bites were developed with martinis in mind! Make a bowl or two for before-dinner nibbles to serve with your favorite before-dinner drinks. Note that they freeze well, so keep some on hand for impromptu entertaining.

Toasted Almonds with Rosemary and Cayenne

8 ounces unblanched almonds or pecan halves (about 2 cups)	1½ teaspoons brown sugar
1½ teaspoons butter or margarine	¼ to ½ teaspoon salt
1 tablespoon finely snipped fresh rosemary	¼ teaspoon cayenne pepper

1. Spread almonds in a single layer on a baking sheet. Bake in a 350°F oven about 10 minutes or until almonds are lightly toasted and fragrant.

2. Meanwhile, in a medium saucepan melt butter over medium heat until bubbly. Remove from heat. Stir in rosemary, brown sugar, salt, and cayenne. Add almonds to butter mixture and toss to coat. Cool slightly before serving. If desired, seal cooled nuts in an airtight container and store for up to 1 month in refrigerator or up to 3 months in freezer. Makes 16 servings.

Classic Cocktails

The cocktail is back! Here's how to make a few of the standbys:

Martini: In a cocktail shaker combine cracked ice, ¼ cup vodka or gin, and a tablespoon of dry vermouth. Shake well to mix. Strain into a chilled cocktail glass. Garnish with a green olive. Makes 1.

Daiquiri: In a cocktail shaker combine cracked ice, 3 tablespoons light rum, 2 tablespoons lime juice, 1 teaspoon powdered sugar, and 1 teaspoon orange liqueur. Shake well to mix; strain into a chilled cocktail glass. Makes 1.

Margarita: In a cocktail shaker combine cracked ice, 3 tablespoons tequila, 2 tablespoons triple sec, and 2 tablespoons lime juice. Shake well to mix. For a salt-rimmed glass, rub the edge of a chilled cocktail glass with a lime wedge; invert into a dish of coarse salt. Strain drink into glass. Makes 1.

Phyllo-Wrapped Brie with Caramelized Onions

1 tablespoon butter or margarine
4 medium onions, cut into thin wedges (about 2 cups)
2 teaspoons sugar
¼ cup chopped hazelnuts (filberts) or walnuts, toasted
8 sheets (17×12 inches) frozen phyllo dough, thawed
¼ cup butter or margarine, melted
2 4½-ounce rounds Brie or Camembert cheese
¼ cup apricot spreadable fruit
Baguette-style French bread slices, pear and/or apple wedges, or assorted crackers

1. In a large saucepan melt the 1 tablespoon butter. Add onion. cook, covered, over medium-low heat about 15 minutes or until onion is tender and golden, stirring occasionally. Sprinkle sugar over onion. Cook, covered, for 10 to 15 minutes more or until brown, stirring occasionally. Stir in hazelnuts; cool.

2. Work with 1 sheet of phyllo at a time, keeping remaining sheets covered with plastic wrap until needed. Lightly brush 1 sheet of phyllo dough with some of the ¼ cup melted butter. Place another sheet of phyllo dough on top of the first sheet, and brush with melted butter. Repeat with 2 more sheets of phyllo, brushing with melted butter. Cut a 12-inch circle from the stack; discard trimmings. Repeat to make a second 12-inch phyllo circle.

3. Slice 1 round of Brie or Camembert in half horizontally. Place bottom half in center of a phyllo circle. Spread cheese with 1 tablespoon of the apricot spreadable fruit; top with one-fourth of the caramelized onion-nut mixture. Top with other cheese half, 1 tablespoon spreadable fruit, and another one-fourth of onion-nut mixture. Wrap phyllo up and over filling, pleating as needed to cover and slightly twisting phyllo on top. Brush phyllo with melted butter. Repeat with remaining phyllo circle, cheese, spreadable fruit, onion-nut mixture, and butter.

4. Place 1 wrapped Brie round in an 8×8×2-inch baking pan or 2 Brie rounds in a 13×9×2-inch baking pan. Cover and chill up to 24 hours. Bake in a 400°F oven about 20 minutes or until golden. Let stand 5 to 10 minutes. Serve with bread, fruit wedges, or crackers. Makes 12 servings.

In the 1990s, restaurants everywhere started wrapping up a small wheel of Brie in a bundle of puff pastry, and we've seen a lot of variations on that theme come through our kitchen ever since. This creative take switches crackly phyllo for the puff pastry for even more contrast between the oozy cheese and its flaky crust. The bonus of caramlized onions makes it pretty special too.

90s

When slow cookers first became popular in the 1970s, we have to admit, we were a bit skeptical. In fact, the Test Kitchen staff had holes drilled into the lids to allow them to insert thermometers—they wanted to make sure food attained safe temperatures during cooking. Since then, we've definitely become slow cooker converts! And while it's hard to choose a favorite slow cooker recipe from the hundreds we've published, this one ranks high for its crowd-pleasing, entertaining angle. Hint: Keep this dip warm in a slow cooker for up to two hours after cooking. Stir just before serving.

Asiago Cheese Dip

1 cup chicken broth or water	1 cup sliced fresh mushrooms
4 ounces dried tomatoes (not oil pack)	1 cup thinly sliced green onions
4 8-ounce cartons dairy sour cream	6 ounces shredded Asiago cheese
1¼ cups mayonnaise	(1½ cups)
½ of an 8-ounce package cream cheese, cut up	Thinly sliced green onions
	Toasted baguette slices

1. In a medium saucepan bring the chicken broth to boiling. Remove from heat and add the dried tomatoes. Cover and let stand for 5 minutes. Drain, discard the liquid, and chop the tomatoes (about 1¼ cups).

2. Meanwhile, in a 3½- to 4-quart slow cooker combine the sour cream, mayonnaise, cream cheese, mushrooms, the 1 cup green onions, and Asiago cheese. Stir in the chopped tomatoes. Cover and cook on low-heat setting for 3 to 4 hours or on high-heat setting for 1½ to 2 hours. Stir before serving and sprinkle with additional green onions. Keep warm on low-heat setting for 1 to 2 hours. Serve warm with toasted baguette slices. Makes 28 servings.

Juliana Hale is the newest member of the Test Kitchen staff, but her connection with our kitchen goes back a long way. "I grew up cooking with the 'red plaid' cookbook," she says; in fact, her mom used to pay her $1 to make dinner, $2 to make bread. Later, she worked as a volunteer cook for a team of geologists using her trusted "red plaid." "An intern told me I should go to chef school," Juli says. "I scoffed at the time, but did just that eight years later." She joined the staff in 2002, just in time to work on the 12th edition of *Better Homes and Gardens New Cook Book*. Today, Juli still loves to bake bread. Try two of her favorites, Orange Bowknots, page 30, and Two-Tone Bread, page 62.

Root Vegetable and Bean Soup

2 medium parsnips, peeled and cut into ½-inch pieces (1½ cups)	1 medium onion, cut into 8 wedges
1 medium potato, cut into ½-inch pieces (1 cup)	1 tablespoon olive oil
	½ teaspoon sea salt or kosher salt
1 small rutabaga, peeled and cut into ½-inch pieces (1 cup)	3 cups vegetable or chicken broth
	1 15-ounce can small red beans, garbanzo beans, or Great Northern beans, rinsed and drained
2 medium carrots, cut into ½-inch slices	2 teaspoons snipped fresh thyme

1. In a large roasting pan toss parsnips, potato, rutabaga, carrots, and onion with oil; sprinkle with salt. Spread the vegetables in a single layer in the roasting pan. Roast in a 450°F oven for 15 to 20 minutes or until the vegetables start to brown.

2. Meanwhile, in a large saucepan bring broth and beans to boiling; add roasted vegetables. Return to boiling; reduce heat. Simmer, covered, about 5 minutes or until vegetables are tender. Stir in thyme. (For a thicker consistency, mash vegetables and beans slightly.) Makes 4 servings.

Maryellyn Krantz joined the Test Kitchen staff in 1973—it was her first job out of college. Thirty years later, she's a true whiz in the kitchen, a knowledgeable pro who can read a recipe and tell if its going to work before she even rolls up her sleeves. And while she's developed a lot of all-out dazzlers in her days, she takes great pleasure in creating honest and reliable family recipes that help real people gather around the table every day. "Bring in the new—but keep the practical," she says. A few of Maryellyn's family-style favorites include Spaghetti Pie, page 97, and Beef and Noodles, page 131.

Underappreciated for decades, the simple technique of roasting has definitely come back into fashion. And the trend isn't just about the Sunday roast either! We love the way roasting adds a caramel color and flavor to fruits and vegetables too. Here root vegetables (also making a culinary comeback) get the royal roasting treatment in this utterly satisfying vegetarian soup.

Marion Viall began her stint in the Test Kitchen in 1959, and she served as its director for 25 years. One of the reasons this ranks among her favorites is that the strawberry and spinach combo was such a refreshing, new idea at the time. And while fruit-studded tossed salads are no longer out of the ordinary, this one with fruit, asparagus, nuts, and turkey still ranks among our best.

Strawberry-Spinach Salad

1   pound asparagus spears
⅓   cup bottled poppy seed salad
      dressing or Italian salad dressing
1   teaspoon finely shredded orange peel
1   tablespoon orange juice
8   cups baby spinach or torn fresh
      spinach

2   cups sliced fresh strawberries and/or
      whole blueberries
¾   to 1 pound cooked turkey, cut into
      ½-inch cubes
¼   cup pecan halves, toasted

1. Snap off and discard woody bases from asparagus. If desired, scrape off scales. Cut into 1-inch pieces. Cook asparagus, covered, in a small amount of boiling lightly salted water for 3 to 5 minutes or until crisp-tender. Drain asparagus. Rinse with cold water. Let stand in cold water until cool; drain.

2. Meanwhile, for dressing, in a small bowl stir together poppy seed dressing, orange peel, and orange juice; set aside.

3. In a salad bowl combine asparagus, spinach, berries, and turkey. Place on salad plates. Top with pecans. Drizzle with dressing. Makes 4 to 6 servings.

Chicken Salad with Peaches, Strawberries, and Glazed Pecans

4 medium skinless, boneless chicken breast halves (about 1½ pounds total), or 1½ pounds turkey tenderloins	3 tablespoons honey
	3 tablespoons peach liqueur
	⅓ cup salad oil
	8 cups torn mixed greens
¼ cup sugar	1½ cups sliced, peeled peaches
¾ cup pecan halves	1½ cups sliced strawberries

1. Place chicken breast halves on the unheated rack of a broiler pan. Broil 4 to 5 inches from the heat for 12 to 15 minutes or until no longer pink (170°F), turning once. Cool; cut into bite-size pieces. Set aside.

2. For glazed pecans, place the sugar in a heavy skillet or saucepan. Cook, without stirring, over medium-high heat until the sugar begins to melt, shaking skillet occasionally. Reduce heat to low. Stir with a wooden spoon until the sugar is golden brown and completely melted; add pecans, stirring to coat. Spread pecans on buttered foil; cool. Break pecans apart.

3. For dressing, in a small mixing bowl combine honey and peach liqueur. Beating with electric mixer on medium speed, add oil in a thin, steady stream. Continue beating for 2 to 3 minutes more or until mixture is thick. Set aside.

4. In a large salad bowl combine chicken pieces, torn mixed greens, peaches, and strawberries. Toss lightly to mix. Pour dressing over salad. Sprinkle with glazed pecans; toss lightly to coat. Divide salad among 4 salad plates. Makes 4 servings.

Here's another recipe in the "Chicken Salad Grows Up" category. The sweet pecans, juicy peaches, and plump strawberries add color to the luncheon salad, while a little honey and peach liqueur add sophistication to the dressing.

Artichoke and Basil Hero

1 cup fresh basil (leaves only)	1 16-ounce loaf unsliced French bread
¼ cup olive oil or salad oil	1 14-ounce can artichoke hearts, drained and sliced
2 tablespoons grated Parmesan cheese	4 ounces sliced provolone cheese
1 tablespoon capers, drained	1 medium tomato, thinly sliced
1 tablespoon white wine vinegar	2 cups torn fresh spinach
2 teaspoons Dijon-style mustard	
1 clove garlic, quartered	

1. In a blender container or food processor bowl combine the basil, oil, Parmesan cheese, capers, vinegar, mustard, and garlic. Cover; blend or process until nearly smooth. Set aside.

2. Cut bread in half lengthwise. Hollow out each half, leaving a ½- to 1-inch shell. (Save bread crumbs for another use.) Spread the basil mixture over cut side of each bread half. On the bottom half, layer artichoke hearts, provolone cheese, tomato, and spinach. Cover with top half of bread. Cut sandwich crosswise into 6 pieces. Makes 6 servings.

While our kitchen has helped to perfect thousands of meatless main-dish recipes, vegetarian cooking is more fun today than ever. The midcentury cook could not easily find basil, capers, or Dijon-style mustard; today, these ingredients and so many more are readily available to make meatless dining—including sandwiches—more interesting than ever.

Here's a peek inside our Test Kitchen Photo Studio, where Senior Food Stylist Charles Worthington, *right*, and Food Stylist Dianna Nolin, *left*, work with editors, art directors, and photographers to create beautiful photographs of our recipes. "my goal is not only to make the food look enticing but to give readers a true representation of what the recipe will look like when they make it at home," says Charlie. Dianna adds that the food readers see in our cookbooks and magazines is very real. "We want the food to appear accessible—not intimidating," she says, "because you *can* do this at home." Two of their favorite recipes for this book included the Mango Buttercream Cake, page 210, and the Pineapple Chiffon Cake, page 38. They're both gorgeous recipes that allowed our stylists' talents to shine.

Spicy Garlic Chicken Pizza

"Fusion" cooking—that is, the bringing together of diverse culinary styles—gained popularity in the 1980s and early '90s. About the same time, chefs and home cooks alike started topping pizzas with ingredients far beyond the realm of mushroom, pepperoni, and green pepper. Here's a cleverly topped, Asia-meets-Italy pizza from 1994 that we fell in love with.

12	ounces skinless, boneless chicken breasts
½	cup sliced green onions
2	cloves garlic, minced
2	tablespoons rice vinegar or white vinegar
2	tablespoons reduced-sodium soy sauce
1	tablespoon olive oil or cooking oil
½	teaspoon crushed red pepper or ¼ teaspoon cayenne pepper
¼	teaspoon black pepper
1	tablespoon olive oil or cooking oil
1	tablespoon cornstarch
1	16-ounce Italian bread shell (Boboli)
½	cup shredded Monterey Jack cheese
½	cup shredded mozzarella cheese
2	tablespoons pine nuts or sliced almonds

1. Cut chicken into ½-inch pieces. In a large bowl combine half of the green onions, the minced garlic, vinegar, soy sauce, 1 tablespoon oil, the red pepper, and black pepper. Add the chicken pieces; stir to coat. Cover and chill for 30 minutes. Drain, reserving liquid.

2. In a large skillet heat the 1 tablespoon oil; add chicken mixture. Cook and stir about 3 minutes or until chicken is no longer pink. Stir cornstarch into reserved liquid. Add to chicken mixture in skillet. Cook and stir until thickened and bubbly.

3. Spoon evenly over bread shell on baking sheet. Sprinkle with Monterey Jack cheese and mozzarella cheese. Bake, uncovered, in a 400°F oven for 12 minutes. Top with remaining green onions and the nuts. Return to oven for 2 minutes more. Cut into wedges to serve. Makes 6 servings.

Pulled Pork with Root Beer Barbecue Sauce

1   2½- to 3-pound pork sirloin roast
½   teaspoon salt
½   teaspoon black pepper
1   tablespoon cooking oil
2   medium onions, cut into thin wedges
1   cup root beer (not diet root beer)
2   tablespoons minced garlic
3   cups root beer (two 12-ounce cans
     or bottles)

1   cup bottled chili sauce
¼   teaspoon root beer concentrate
     (optional)
     Several dashes bottled hot pepper
     sauce (optional)
8   to 10 hamburger buns, split and
     toasted
     Lettuce leaves (optional)
     Tomato slices (optional)

1. Trim fat from meat. If necessary, cut roast to fit into slow cooker. Sprinkle meat with salt and pepper. In a large skillet heat oil over medium-high heat. Brown roast on all sides in hot oil. Drain off fat. Transfer meat to a 3½-, 4-, or 5-quart electric slow cooker. Add onions, the 1 cup root beer, and garlic. Cover and cook on low-heat setting for 8 to 10 hours or on high-heat setting for 4 to 5 hours.

2. Meanwhile, for sauce, in a medium saucepan combine the 3 cups root beer and the chili sauce. Bring to boiling; reduce heat. Boil gently, uncovered, about 30 minutes or until mixture is reduced to 2 cups, stirring occasionally. If desired, add ¼ teaspoon root beer concentrate and several dashes hot pepper sauce.

3. Transfer roast to a cutting board or serving platter. Using a slotted spoon, remove onions from juices and place on serving platter. Discard juices. Using 2 forks, pull meat apart into shreds. To serve, if desired, line bottom halves of buns with lettuce leaves and sliced tomatoes. Add meat and onions; spoon on sauce. Add bun tops. Makes 8 to 10 servings.

Root beer in barbecue sauce? It works here, giving these pork sandwiches a rich color and pleasant sweetness. Readers must think it's a pretty special recipe too, as we've had a lot of requests for it since it was published in 1998. Hint: Find root beer concentrate in the spice section of large supermarkets.

Pesto-Stuffed Pork Chops

What did we ever do without pesto? While traditionally a sauce for pasta, these days it adds flavor to just about everything except dessert! Here, this contemporary convenience product is combined with feta cheese and pine nuts to make a flavorful filling for grilled pork chops.

3 tablespoons crumbled feta cheese	1 teaspoon dried oregano, crushed
2 tablespoons refrigerated basil pesto	1 teaspoon bottled minced garlic (2 cloves)
1 tablespoon pine nuts, toasted	¼ teaspoon crushed red pepper
4 pork loin chops or boneless pork loin chops, cut 1¼ inches thick	¼ teaspoon dried thyme, crushed
1 teaspoon freshly ground black pepper	1 tablespoon balsamic vinegar

1. For filling, in a small bowl stir together the feta cheese, pesto, and pine nuts. Set aside.

2. Trim fat from meat. To make a pocket in each chop, use a sharp knife to make a 2-inch slit in the fatty side. Work knife through chop, cutting almost through to the opposite side, and keeping the original slit as narrow as possible. Spoon filling into each pocket. If necessary, secure the opening with a wooden toothpick.

3. For rub, in a small bowl combine black pepper, oregano, garlic, red pepper, and thyme. Rub evenly onto all sides of meat. Place chops on a rack in a shallow roasting pan. Bake in a 375°F oven for 35 to 45 minutes or until done (160°F). Brush vinegar onto chops the last 5 minutes of baking. Remove and discard toothpicks before serving. Makes 4 servings.

Jill Moberly oversees testing for a variety of special projects, including annual publications such as, *Christmas Cooking from the Heart* and *Celebrate the Seasons*—topics in sync with her love for party foods. "We live in a neighborhood with lots of young families," Jill says, "so our weekend nights consist of casual get-togethers." Among Jill's favorite munchies to share with her neighbors: Caramel Crunch Corn, page 76, and Asiago Cheese Dip, page 188. In fact, Jill developed the slow cooker version of this great dip.

Citrus Herb Pork Roast

1 2- to 3-pound boneless pork top loin
   roast (single loin)
3 tablespoons frozen orange juice
   concentrate, thawed
1 teaspoon finely shredded lime peel
3 tablespoons lime juice

1 tablespoon cooking oil
2 cloves garlic, minced
1½ teaspoons dried oregano, crushed
½ teaspoon black pepper
⅛ teaspoon salt

1. Place meat in a large plastic bag set in a large, deep bowl. For marinade, combine thawed orange juice concentrate, lime peel, lime juice, oil, garlic, oregano, pepper, and salt. Pour marinade over the meat; seal bag. Marinate in the refrigerator at least 4 hours or overnight, turning meat and bag several times.

2. Drain meat, discarding marinade. Place the meat on a rack in a shallow roasting pan. Insert an oven-going thermometer into center of roast. Roast in a 325°F oven for 1¼ to 1¾ hours or until meat thermometer registers 155°F. Cover roast; let stand for 15 minutes before slicing. The temperature of the meat after standing should be 160°F. Makes 6 to 8 servings.

Colleen Weeden inherited her love of cooking from her father, who canned his own vegetables from the garden, fixed pancakes every Sunday, and made a mean batch of cinnamon rolls. Now, Colleen, mother of three, is especially interested in the bond between food and family, and enjoys passing on food traditions to the next generation of cooks. For a great kid-friendly recipe, see Bar-B-Que Burgers, page 52, a sandwich that not only won favor in our Test Kitchen, but also passed with flying colors at her own family's table.

Test Kitchen Director

Lynn Blanchard recommends this lively pork roast for entertaining family and friends. The spicy-citrus flavors reflect those found in Caribbean cooking, which has recently gained popularity. For a Cuban-style relish, stir together a carton of guacamole with a bit of diced fresh pineapple.

Pork Medaillons with Fennel and Pancetta

During the '90s, informal neighborhood bistros started to pop up all over the country, and soon home cooks were emulating the fresh, simple, and lively fare found in these bustling venues. In this bistro-style dish, the ingredients with wow-power are fennel, which adds licoricelike tones, and pancetta, a flavorful Italian bacon. A touch of cream only makes it that much more irresistible.

1	12-ounce pork tenderloin	2	fennel bulbs, trimmed and cut crosswise into ¼-inch slices
¼	cup all-purpose flour	1	small onion, thinly sliced
	Dash salt	2	cloves garlic, minced
	Dash pepper	2	tablespoons lemon juice
2	tablespoons olive oil	½	cup whipping cream
2	ounces pancetta (Italian bacon) or bacon, finely chopped		

1. Trim fat from meat. Cut meat crosswise into 1-inch slices. Place each slice between 2 pieces of plastic wrap. Pound meat lightly with the flat side of a meat mallet to a ¼-inch thickness. Remove plastic wrap. Combine flour, salt, and pepper in a shallow dish. Dip meat slices in flour mixture to coat.

2. Heat oil in a large heavy skillet over high heat. Add meat, half at a time, and cook for 2 to 3 minutes or until meat is slightly pink in center, turning once. (Add more oil, if necessary.) Remove meat from skillet; set aside and keep warm.

3. Cook pancetta in the same skillet over medium-high heat until crisp. Add fennel, onion, and garlic; cook for 3 to 5 minutes or until crisp-tender. Add lemon juice; stir in whipping cream. Bring to boiling; return meat to pan. Cook until meat is heated through and sauce is slightly thickened. Transfer the meat to a serving platter. Spoon the sauce over the meat. Makes 4 servings.

Creamy Tomato Pasta with Pine Nuts

1 9-ounce package refrigerated linguine
3 ounces pancetta or bacon, finely chopped
2 cups sliced fresh mushrooms
½ cup pine nuts
1 tablespoon butter or margarine
1½ cups half-and-half or light cream
¼ teaspoon coarsely ground black pepper

2 medium tomatoes or 4 plum tomatoes, peeled, seeded, and chopped (about 1¾ cups)
½ cup freshly grated Parmesan cheese
Coarsely ground black pepper (optional)
Freshly grated Parmesan cheese (optional)

1. Cook linguine according to package directions. Drain and keep warm.

2. Meanwhile, in a large skillet cook and stir pancetta just until golden. Remove from skillet; drain off fat. In the same skillet cook mushrooms and pine nuts in hot butter until mushrooms are tender and pine nuts are golden. Return pancetta to skillet. Stir in half-and-half and the ¼ teaspoon pepper. Bring to boiling; reduce heat. Boil gently, uncovered, about 7 minutes over medium heat or until mixture thickens slightly. Stir in chopped tomatoes.

3. Toss hot cooked pasta with the ½ cup Parmesan cheese. Add to tomato mixture; toss lightly to coat. If desired, sprinkle with additional pepper and Parmesan cheese. Makes 4 servings.

Bow Ties with Olives and Mint

8 ounces dried bow tie pasta	½ cup snipped fresh mint
¾ cup Greek black olives, pitted and halved, or ripe olives, halved	2 tablespoons olive oil
	¼ teaspoon black pepper
2 plum tomatoes, seeded and chopped	
¾ cup crumbled feta cheese or soft goat cheese (chèvre) (3 ounces)	

1. Cook pasta according to package directions; drain.

2. Meanwhile, in a large bowl combine olives, tomatoes, cheese, and mint. Add pasta, olive oil, and pepper; toss gently to combine. Serve pasta mixture immediately. Makes 4 servings.

Lori Wilson joined the Test Kitchen in 1984. While she's cooked just about everything in her nearly 20 years in the kitchen, she loves to bake. And though she's a seasoned food professional, Lori's love for baking is, at heart, little different from that of most people who love to bake. "I simply enjoy how much pleasure it gives my family and friends when I prepare something special for them," she says. When you're looking to prepare something special for your family and friends, try Pecan Crispies page 73, and Creamy Ham and Egg Bake, page 128, two of Lori's favorites.

Once fresh herbs became readily available, they became widely used in our recipes. In fact, these days, they're almost considered a "convenience product," as few other ingredients add so much flavor with so little effort. We love this recipe because it melds garden-fresh ingredients—the mint and tomatoes—with staples that are easy to keep on hand. So head to the farmer's market (or out to the garden) and come inside for a wonderfully summery and simple meal in minutes.

As Americans began to appreciate a fresher, more authentic side of Mexican and Southwestern cooking, cilantro became a mainstream ingredient. Cilantro, cumin, and lime juice bring a Southwest update to the traditional three-bean salad.

Southwestern-Style Three-Bean Salad

1 15-ounce can garbanzo beans, rinsed and drained
1 15-ounce can black beans, rinsed and drained
1 15-ounce can red kidney beans, rinsed and drained
1 cup thinly sliced celery
¾ cup chopped red onion
¼ cup salad oil

¼ cup vinegar
2 tablespoons snipped fresh cilantro
2 tablespoons lime juice
1 tablespoon sugar
1 clove garlic, minced
½ teaspoon chili powder
½ teaspoon ground cumin
¼ teaspoon salt

1. In a large bowl stir together the garbanzo beans, black beans, red kidney beans, celery, and onion.

2. For dressing, in a screw-top jar combine the salad oil, vinegar, cilantro, lime juice, sugar, garlic, chili powder, cumin, and salt. Cover and shake well.

3. Pour dressing over bean mixture; toss to coat. Cover and chill for 3 to 24 hours, stirring occasionally. Serve with a slotted spoon. Makes 8 servings.

Basil Tortellini Salad

1   9-ounce package refrigerated cheese
     tortellini
1   small red sweet pepper, cut into
     bite-size strips
1   cup broccoli florets
¾   cup thinly sliced carrot (1 large)
½   cup mayonnaise or salad dressing
2   tablespoons grated Parmesan cheese

3   tablespoons snipped fresh basil
1   tablespoon milk
½   teaspoon freshly ground black pepper
1   clove garlic, minced
2   tablespoons pine nuts or chopped
     walnuts, toasted (optional)
    Milk (optional)

1. Cook pasta according to package directions; drain pasta. Rinse pasta with cold water; drain again. In a large bowl combine pasta, sweet pepper, broccoli, and carrot.

2. For dressing, in a small bowl stir together mayonnaise, Parmesan cheese, basil, milk, black pepper, and garlic. Pour the dressing over the pasta mixture. Toss lightly to coat. Cover and chill for 4 to 24 hours. Before serving, stir in nuts, if desired. If necessary, add milk to moisten. Makes 6 servings.

We were pretty excited when refrigerated tortellini started appearing in mainstream supermarkets everywhere. And when fresh basil finally became abundant, this recipe was a shoo-in for a stylish, fresh-focused replacement to the everyday pasta salad. It still makes perfect picnic fare.

Every cook needs a "little black dress" of side dishes—something simple and great that goes with just about anything. We especially like this version of risotto because while it has the characteristically creamy texture of risotto, the constant stirring required by the more classic dish is eliminated. For a light supper in summer, go with the peas option, then sprinkle it with fresh herbs from the garden, and serve with a salad of sliced tomatoes, fresh mozzarella, and basil leaves drizzled with olive oil.

Easy Risotto

⅓ cup chopped onion
1 tablespoon butter or margarine
⅔ cup uncooked arborio or long grain rice
2 cups water
1 teaspoon instant chicken bouillon granules

Dash black pepper
1 cup frozen peas (optional)
¼ cup grated Parmesan or Romano cheese

1. In a medium saucepan cook onion in hot butter until tender; add rice. Cook and stir for 2 minutes more. Carefully stir in water, bouillon granules, and pepper. Bring to boiling; reduce heat. Simmer, covered, for 20 minutes (do not lift cover).

2. Remove saucepan from heat. If desired, stir in peas. Let stand, covered, for 5 minutes. Rice should be tender but slightly firm, and the mixture should be creamy. (If necessary, stir in a little water to reach desired consistency.) Stir in Parmesan cheese. Makes 3 to 4 servings.

Jennifer Kalinowski's passion for food started at a young age. She recalls watching cooking shows on TV as a young girl. While her friends were outside playing, Jennifer was busy in the kitchen. Now a registered dietitian with a master's degree in public health, she oversees recipe testing for many of our health- and nutrition-related publications. One of her favorite recipes in this book is Frisky Sours, page 84, which taps into today's "everything in moderation" credo. The Overnight Three-Grain Waffles, page 141, and Cheddar Squash Bake, page 59, are close seconds.

Gingerbread Scones

2	cups all-purpose flour	¼	cup butter
3	tablespoons packed brown sugar	1	beaten egg yolk
2	teaspoons baking powder	⅓	cup molasses
1	teaspoon ground ginger	¼	cup milk
½	teaspoon baking soda	1	slightly beaten egg white
½	teaspoon ground cinnamon		Coarse sugar (optional)
⅛	teaspoon salt		Nutmeg Whipped Cream (optional)

1. In a large bowl stir together the flour, brown sugar, baking powder, ginger, baking soda, cinnamon, and salt. Using a pastry blender, cut in butter until mixture resembles coarse crumbs. Make a well in the center of the flour mixture; set aside.

2. In a small bowl combine the egg yolk, molasses, and milk. Add egg yolk mixture all at once to flour mixture. Using a fork, stir just until moistened.

3. Turn the dough out onto a lightly floured surface. Quickly knead the dough for 10 to 12 strokes or until nearly smooth. Pat or lightly roll dough into a 9×7-inch rectangle. Cut into 8 rectangles. Place rectangles 1 inch apart on an ungreased baking sheet. Brush with egg white and, if desired, sprinkle with coarse sugar.

4. Bake in a 400°F oven about 12 minutes or until bottoms are brown. Remove from baking sheet; cool slightly on a wire rack. Serve warm. If desired, serve with Nutmeg Whipped Cream. Makes 8 scones.

Nutmeg Whipped Cream: In a chilled small mixing bowl combine ½ cup whipping cream, 1 tablespoon sugar, ¼ teaspoon finely shredded orange peel, ¼ teaspoon vanilla, and ⅛ teaspoon ground nutmeg. Beat with chilled beaters of an electric mixer on medium speed until soft peaks form (tips curl). Serve immediately or cover and refrigerate up to 2 hours. Makes 1 cup.

Make-ahead directions: Prepare and bake Gingerbread Scones as directed; cool. Wrap tightly in foil; place in a freezer bag. Freeze up to 3 months. Up to 2 hours ahead, prepare Nutmeg Whipped Cream; cover and refrigerate. To serve, reheat foil-wrapped frozen scones in a 300°F oven for 15 to 20 minutes or until warm (if thawed, reheat for 10 to 15 minutes).

Scones are similar to drop cookies—the variations on the theme seem endless! Here's a great gingery take on this quintessential teatime treat, chosen from the dozens in our archives.

No cookbook of our all-time favorites would be complete without a great recipe for cinnamon rolls. The dried fruit bits add an extra something special to the mix. And if you're not inclined to make bread dough from scratch, you can still treat your family to this home-baked treat—just use frozen bread dough in place of the homemade dough and begin with step 3 of the recipe.

Maple-Nut Rolls

4¼ to 4¾ cups all-purpose flour	¼ cup all-purpose flour
1 package active dry yeast	1 tablespoon apple pie spice
1 cup milk	¼ cup butter
⅓ cup butter	1 cup finely snipped dried apricots
⅓ cup granulated sugar	½ cup chopped toasted pecans
½ teaspoon salt	2 to 4 tablespoons half-and-half or
3 eggs	light cream
¾ cup packed brown sugar	Maple Glaze

1. In a large mixing bowl stir together 2¼ cups of the flour and the yeast. In a saucepan heat and stir milk, the ⅓ cup butter, granulated sugar, and salt just until warm (120°F to 130°F) and butter almost melts. Add milk mixture to flour mixture along with eggs. Beat with an electric mixer on low speed for 30 seconds, scraping bowl. Beat on high speed for 3 minutes. Stir in as much of the remaining flour from the 4¼ to 4¾ cups as you can.

2. Turn dough out onto a lightly floured surface. Knead in enough of the flour remaining from the 4¼ to 4¾ cups to make a moderately soft dough that is smooth and elastic (3 to 5 minutes total). Shape into a ball. Place in a greased bowl, turning once to grease surface of dough. Cover; let rise in a warm place until double in size (about 1 hour).

3. Punch dough down. Turn out onto a lightly floured surface. Divide in half. Cover; let rest for 10 minutes. Meanwhile, lightly grease 2 pans (15×10×1-inch and/or 13×9×2-inch). Roll each half of dough into a 12×8-inch rectangle.

4. For filling, combine brown sugar, the ¼ cup flour, and apple pie spice. Using a pastry blender, cut in the ¼ cup butter until crumbly. Stir in dried apricots. Sprinkle filling over dough rectangles; top with pecans. Roll each rectangle into a spiral starting from a long side. Seal seams. Slice each spiral into 12 pieces. Place rolls, cut sides down, in prepared pans.

5. Cover rolls loosely with clear plastic wrap, leaving room for rolls to rise. Refrigerate for 2 to 24 hours. Uncover rolls; let stand at room temperature for 30 minutes. (To bake rolls right away, don't chill dough. Instead, cover loosely; let rolls rise in a warm place until nearly double, about 30 minutes.) Break any surface bubbles with a greased toothpick. Brush rolls with some of the half-and-half. Bake in a 375°F oven for 18 to 20 minutes for 15×10×1-inch pan or 20 to 22 minutes for a 13×9×2-inch pan or until bottoms are lightly browned. (If necessary, cover rolls loosely with foil for the last 5 to 10 minutes of baking to prevent overbrowning.) Remove from oven. Brush again with half-and-half. Cool for 1 minute. Carefully transfer rolls to a wire rack. Cool slightly. Drizzle with Maple Glaze. Serve warm. Makes 24 rolls.

Maple Glaze: Melt 3 tablespoons butter in a small saucepan; heat over medium-low heat for 7 to 10 minutes or until light brown; remove from heat. Stir in 1½ cups sifted powdered sugar and ¼ cup maple syrup or maple-flavored syrup. If needed, stir in milk to make of drizzling consistency.

Chocolatey Bourbon and Nut Pie

1	recipe Pastry for Single-Crust Pie	⅛	teaspoon salt
3	eggs, slightly beaten	½	cup finely chopped pecans
¾	cup light-color corn syrup	⅓	cup bourbon
3	tablespoons granulated sugar	1	cup semisweet chocolate pieces
3	tablespoons packed brown sugar		(6 ounces)
3	tablespoons butter, softened	1⅓	cups pecan halves
1	teaspoon vanilla		

1. Prepare Pastry for Single-Crust Pie. On a lightly floured surface, roll dough from center to edges into a circle about 12 inches in diameter. Line a 9-inch pie plate with the pastry. Trim to ½ inch beyond edge. Fold under extra pastry and flute edge. Do not prick pastry.

2. For filling, in a large bowl combine the eggs, corn syrup, granulated sugar, brown sugar, butter, vanilla, and salt; mix well. Stir in the chopped pecans and bourbon.

3. Lightly pat chocolate pieces onto bottom of pastry shell. Pour filling over chocolate pieces. Arrange pecan halves on filling.

4. Bake in a 350°F oven for 45 to 60 minutes or until a knife inserted near the center comes out clean. Cover edges of pie loosely with foil the last 30 minutes to prevent overbrowning. Makes 10 servings.

Pastry for Single-Crust Pie: Stir together 1¼ cups all-purpose flour and ¼ teaspoon salt. Using a pastry blender, cut in ⅓ cup shortening until pieces are pea-size. Sprinkle 1 tablespoon cold water over part of mixture; gently toss with a fork. Push moistened dough to side of bowl. Repeat, using 1 tablespoon of water at a time, until flour mixture is moistened (4 to 5 tablespoons total). Form dough into a ball.

At taste panels, we rarely eat an entire serving of everything being tested; we pace ourselves, knowing there's more to come. We must admit, however, that all restraint was lost when tasting this luscious treat—a pecan pie with a bonus layer of chocolate and a hint of bourbon. Published in 1996, this dessert is also a reader favorite.

Chippers in a Jar

¾ cup all-purpose flour
½ teaspoon baking soda
⅓ cup granulated sugar
⅓ cup packed brown sugar
1 cup semisweet chocolate pieces
1 cup rolled oats
½ cup peanut butter pieces
½ cup butter, softened
1 slightly beaten egg
1 teaspoon vanilla

1. Stir together flour and baking soda in a small bowl. In a 1-quart glass jar or canister layer the following ingredients, gently tapping the jar on the counter to settle each layer before adding the next: granulated sugar, brown sugar, chocolate pieces, oats, flour mixture, and peanut butter pieces. Cover the jar.

2. Store at room temperature for up to 1 month. Or attach baking directions and give as gift. Makes 24 to 30 cookies.

Baking directions: Empty contents of jar into a large bowl. Add ½ cup butter, softened; 1 beaten egg; and 1 teaspoon vanilla. Stir until combined. Drop dough by heaping teaspoons 2 inches apart onto a greased cookie sheet. Bake in a 375°F oven for 8 to 10 minutes or until edges are lightly browned. Transfer cookies to a wire rack to cool.

Judging from the number of requests we get for "cookies in a jar" recipes, this idea is a favorite among people who like to give food gifts. Recipients likely love the concept too—the mix lets them bake a batch of homemade cookies whenever they wish.

While methods of cooking macaroons vary widely, we've toyed with them enough to know what it takes to concoct an incredibly luscious confection. Our best-ever version starts with mixing two kinds of coconut, regular flaked sweetened coconut from the grocery and unsweetened finely shredded coconut from the health food store, for a macaroon with pleasing texture and a well-rounded flavor that's not overly sweet. We also find a touch of honey promotes a golden brown crust of toasted coconut, deepening the flavor. P.S. This is a favorite of Lynn Blanchard, the current Test Kitchen Director.

Golden Macaroons

2½	cups flaked sweetened coconut (about 7 ounces)	3 tablespoons all-purpose flour
2	cups unsweetened finely shredded coconut	¼ teaspoon salt
1	cup sugar	4 egg whites
		1 tablespoon honey
		1 teaspoon vanilla

1. In a large bowl combine flaked and shredded coconut until evenly mixed. (Flaked coconut should be broken into separate flakes with only a few very small clumps present.)

2. In a medium bowl combine sugar, flour, and salt. Add egg whites, honey, and vanilla. Whisk rapidly until smooth. Pour sugar mixture over coconut mixture. Stir with a wooden spoon, then use your hands to blend until evenly mixed. Cover with plastic wrap; chill for 30 minutes.

3. Line a large cookie sheet with parchment paper. Drop rounded tablespoons of macaroon batter onto the cookie sheet about 2 inches apart. Gently pinch mounds into shaggy pyramids. Bake in a 300°F oven for 17 to 19 minutes or until golden brown. Immediately transfer macaroons to a wire rack to cool. Makes 24 macaroons.

Chocolate Macaroon Sandwiches: Loosely pack macaroon dough in tablespoons. Transfer spoonfuls to parchment-lined cookie sheet; press gently to form flattened mounds. Bake in a 300°F oven for 20 to 22 minutes; cool. In a small saucepan heat ¾ cup heavy cream to near boiling; remove from heat. Add 6 ounces chopped semisweet chocolate. Let stand 5 minutes, then whisk until smooth. Cool completely. Make sandwiches by spooning a mound of chocolate mixture onto bottom of half the macaroons. Top each with second macaroon and gently press the layers together. Makes about 12 sandwiches.

Chocolate Chunk Cookies

2 ounces unsweetened chocolate, chopped	2 cups all-purpose flour
1 cup butter, softened	6 ounces white baking bar, cut into chunks
¾ cup granulated sugar	6 ounces semisweet or bittersweet chocolate, cut into chunks
¾ cup packed brown sugar	1 cup chopped walnuts or pecans (optional)
1 teaspoon baking soda	
2 eggs	
1 teaspoon vanilla	

1. Place unsweetened chocolate in a heavy small saucepan. Cook and stir over very low heat until chocolate is melted. Set aside to cool.

2. In a large mixing bowl beat butter with an electric mixer on medium to high speed for 30 seconds. Add the cooled chocolate, granulated sugar, brown sugar, and baking soda. Beat until combined, scraping sides of bowl. Beat in eggs and vanilla until combined. Gradually beat in flour. Stir in the white baking bar and semisweet chocolate chunks and, if desired, nuts.

3. Drop by rounded tablespoons 3 inches apart on an ungreased cookie sheet. Bake in a 375°F oven for 9 to 11 minutes or until edges are firm. Cool on a cookie sheet for 1 minute. Transfer cookies to a wire rack to cool. Makes about 45 cookies.

Test Kitchen pro Marilyn Cornelius, who recently celebrated her 30th year in the kitchen, ranks these among her favorites. They're as easy as any drop cookie, but the triple hit of chocolate makes them a heaven-sent treat for the serious chocolate lover (and Marilyn definitely considers herself a member of that club).

The longest-reigning member of the current Test Kitchen staff, Marilyn Cornelius started working in the Test Kitchen just out of college, in 1972. While she can cook just about anything, she enjoys making yeast breads and is also a big fan of chocolate (try two of her favorites—Creamy, Fudgy and Nutty Brownies, *right*, and Chocolate Chunk Cookies, *above*). She's also famous in the kitchen for perfecting the Baumkuchen recipe on page 214—an impressive, intricately layered Swiss-German pastry. It remains one of our favorite dazzlers today.

Creamy, Fudgy, and Nutty Brownies

4 ounces unsweetened chocolate, chopped	1 teaspoon vanilla
½ cup butter	3 ounces semisweet or bittersweet chocolate, chopped
1 cup all-purpose flour	2 3-ounce packages cream cheese, softened
½ cup chopped walnuts or pecans, toasted	1 egg
¼ teaspoon baking powder	¼ cup sugar
1½ cups sugar	1 tablespoon milk
3 eggs	½ teaspoon vanilla

1. Grease an 8×8×2-inch baking pan; set aside. In a small saucepan melt the unsweetened chocolate and butter over low heat, stirring occasionally. Remove from heat; set aside to cool slightly. In a medium bowl stir together the flour, walnuts, and baking powder; set aside.

2. In a large bowl stir together the melted chocolate mixture and the 1½ cups sugar. Add the 3 eggs and 1 teaspoon vanilla. Using a wooden spoon, lightly beat just until combined. (Do not overbeat or brownies will rise during baking, then fall and crack.) Stir in the flour mixture. Spread the batter in the prepared pan. Bake in a 350°F oven for 40 minutes.

3. Meanwhile, for topping, in a small saucepan melt semisweet chocolate over low heat, stirring constantly; cool slightly. In a medium mixing bowl beat the cream cheese with an electric mixer on medium speed about 30 seconds or until softened. Add the melted semisweet chocolate, the 1 egg, the ¼ cup sugar, the milk, and the ½ teaspoon vanilla. Beat until combined.

4. Carefully spread topping evenly over hot brownies. Bake 10 to 12 minutes more or until the topping is set. Cool brownies in pan on a wire rack. Cover and chill in the refrigerator for at least 2 hours before serving. To serve, cut into bars. Cover; refrigerate to store. Makes 16 brownies.

Does a brownie rate as a spectacular dessert? This one does! It appeared in the 1992 book *Spectacular Desserts*, which rounded up the ultimate feast in sweets. Kicking off the book were our favorite chocolate indulgences, including this showstopping brownie. Just add a dollop of whipped cream and a sprinkling of grated chocolate, and you'll have pure decadance.

One of the great pleasures of working in a test kitchen is coming upon a fresh, new variation of a tried-and-true classic. For example, just when you think you've seen about every interesting take on fudge there could possibly be, in comes another great idea—this one with a luscious honey and buttery macadamia nut angle. It's a terrific choice for gift-giving any time of year.

Honey-Macadamia Nut Fudge

Butter
1½ cups granulated sugar
1 cup packed brown sugar
⅓ cup half-and-half or light cream
⅓ cup milk
2 tablespoons honey
2 tablespoons butter

1 teaspoon vanilla
½ cup coarsely chopped macadamia nuts, hazelnuts (filberts), or pecans
36 Chocolate-Dipped Nuts or additional chopped nuts (optional)*

1. Line an 8×8×2-inch baking pan with foil, extending foil over edges of the pan. Butter the foil; set aside.

2. Butter the sides of a heavy 2-quart straight-sided saucepan. (If your saucepan has a very wide diameter, cooking times will be shorter.) In the saucepan, combine the granulated sugar, brown sugar, half-and-half, milk, and honey. Cook over medium-high heat to boiling, stirring constantly with a wooden spoon to dissolve sugars. This should take about 8 minutes. Avoid splashing mixture on sides of the pan. Carefully clip a candy thermometer to the side of the saucepan.

3. Cook over medium-low heat, stirring frequently, until thermometer registers 236°F, soft-ball stage. Mixture should boil at a moderate, steady rate over the entire surface. Reaching soft-ball stage should take 15 to 20 minutes. Remove saucepan from heat. Add the 2 tablespoons butter and the vanilla, but do not stir. Cool, without stirring, to lukewarm (110°F). This should take 45 to 50 minutes.

4. Remove candy thermometer from saucepan. Beat vigorously with the wooden spoon until fudge begins to thicken. Add coarsely chopped nuts. Continue beating until mixture is very thick and just starts to lose its gloss. This should take about 10 minutes total.

5. Quickly turn fudge into prepared pan. While fudge is warm, score it into 1¼-inch squares. When fudge is firm, use foil to lift it out of pan; cut into squares. Tightly cover and store in a cool, dry place. If desired, top with Chocolate-Dipped Nuts or additional chopped nuts.

*Chocolate-Dipped Nuts: In a small saucepan melt ½ cup semisweet chocolate pieces and 1 teaspoon shortening over low heat. Add 36 whole macadamia nuts, hazelnuts, or pecan halves. Stir to coat. Remove with a fork, allowing excess chocolate to drip off. Place on a baking sheet lined with waxed paper. Allow to stand until set.

1928

OUR FAVORITE
Showstoppers

2003

Many great times have been featured on the pages of *Better Homes and Gardens* magazines and books. It's true— we love a party! Come take a look at the fun we've had throughout the decades. When it's time to gather friends and family for a special occasion, choose from our favorite selection of showstopping party fare, pick up the phone, and let the good times continue.

Parties on our pages

1950-60s: Thanks to America's new-found love for foreign foods and more money in the family budget, entertaining got a little fancier in the '50s and '60s. But that doesn't mean we didn't have a few tricks for keeping things easy on the cook. At this stylish party, featured in a 1959 cookbook, the advice was to "Consider self service—the buffet, luau, and smorgasboard rate high with every hostess who likes to enjoy her own party. All the flurry is over before guests arrive." Buffets are still one of our favorite fuss-free ways to serve a crowd.

50/60s

1930s

1930s: Here's an idea from March 1937: Set aside one night a week for company. According to the author, the plan has "all the pepping-up quality of a new hat or a business bonus!" The trick is to keep it simple—serve a family supper dressed up with a trick or two. The advantages are many: "It's really doing things to us as a family," wrote the author. "We're closer knit, more interested in each other, less inclined to think of home merely as a roosting place between mad dashes here and there."

1940s

1940s: Encompassing the war years followed by the start of the baby boom, our focus in the '40s was more about thrifty oven meals and feeding the family than about giving grand and glamorous parties. But when it did come time to entertain, the message in this January 1947 story was, once again, to keep it simple. "Notice how folks relax, have more fun at your house, when you entertain casually without a lot of fuss?" More than 50 years later, we're still singing the same tune.

1990s to Now: Entertaining has come full circle—and is better for the journey. Thanks to today's wonderful array of fresh produce and exciting global ingredients, stylish, rave-worthy foods can be prepared more easily than ever. This title, published in 1998, combines the current focus on freshness with the "keep it simple" attitude of earlier decades. Best of all, the focus is on the "friends" part of entertaining, not the fuss.

1970s: "The starched and stuffy sit-down dinner is out!" exclaimed this story in November 1977. "Welcome the stylish meal that puts the accent on people, not pomp." It's true. "No hassles!" was the entertaining mantra of the laid-back '70s, when a party was defined simply as what happens when good friends get together. We've been creating stylish, yet simple, recipes that keep the focus on fun ever since.

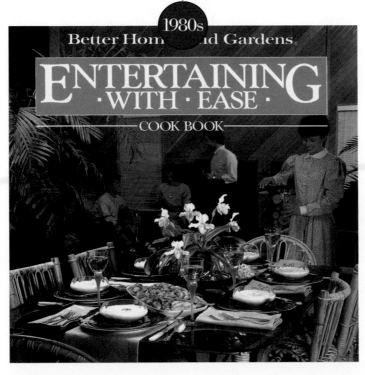

1980s: High-end entertaining came into fashion for a while in the gourmet food-loving '80s, and the "dress for success" attitude of the era made its way to the table, with beautifully plated upscale food presented on stylishly wrought tables. And yet, while this 1984 title was chock-full of great gourmet ideas from soufflés to canapes, it also contained plenty of recipes for easygoing good times, from picnics to soup suppers. The focus was, after all, on "Entertaining with Ease"—a legacy leftover from the '70s.

Salmon Mousse

1 14³⁄₄- to 15¹⁄₂-ounce can red salmon	2 hard-cooked eggs, chopped
2 envelopes unflavored gelatin	2 tablespoons snipped chives
1 teaspoon sugar	¹⁄₄ teaspoon black pepper
1¹⁄₄ cups mayonnaise or salad dressing	¹⁄₂ cup whipping cream
¹⁄₄ cup tomato sauce	Lettuce (optional)
2 tablespoons lemon juice	Thin cucumber slices
2 teaspoons Worcestershire sauce	Fresh dill
¹⁄₂ cup finely chopped celery	Assorted crackers

1. Drain salmon, reserving the liquid. Bone and flake salmon; set aside. Add enough water to the reserved salmon liquid to equal 1 cup; pour into a small saucepan. Sprinkle unflavored gelatin and sugar over the salmon liquid mixture; let stand 3 minutes to soften gelatin. Heat, stirring constantly, over medium-low heat until gelatin dissolves. Remove from heat.

2. In a large bowl combine mayonnaise, tomato sauce, lemon juice, and Worcestershire sauce; stir in gelatin mixture. Chill until partially set, about 30 minutes. Fold in salmon, celery, chopped hard-cooked eggs, chives, and pepper.

3. In a chilled small mixing bowl beat whipping cream until soft peaks form. Fold whipped cream into gelatin mixture. Pour into a 6-cup fish-shape or ring mold. Cover and chill until firm, about 4 hours. To serve, line a tray or serving plate with lettuce, if desired. Unmold mousse onto tray. Garnish with cucumber slices and fresh dill. Serve with assorted crackers. Makes 16 servings.

Baked Appetizer Crepes

12 6-inch Basic Crepes	½ cup grated Parmesan cheese
2 beaten eggs	¼ teaspoon black pepper
2 cups ricotta cheese (15 ounces)	Dash garlic powder
1½ cups shredded Swiss cheese (6 ounces)	½ cup butter
	1 cup whipping cream
1 10-ounce package frozen chopped spinach, thawed and well drained	½ cup grated Parmesan cheese
1½ cups soft bread crumbs (3 slices bread)	

1. Prepare Basic Crepes. In a mixing bowl combine eggs, ricotta, Swiss cheese, spinach, bread crumbs, ½ cup Parmesan cheese, pepper, and garlic powder; mix well. Spoon about ⅓ cup filling into center of each crepe; roll up. Cut each rolled crepe crosswise into thirds. Place the pieces, cut sides up, in a 2-quart baking dish (placing pieces close together will help them remain upright).

2. In a small saucepan melt butter; stir in cream and ½ cup Parmesan cheese. Cook and stir over medium heat until mixture thickens slightly. Pour the sauce over crepes. Bake in a 400°F oven for 18 to 20 minutes or until heated through. Makes 36 appetizer servings.

Basic Crepes: In a medium mixing bowl combine 2 beaten eggs, 1½ cups milk, 1 cup all-purpose flour, 1 tablespoon cooking oil, and ¼ teaspoon salt; beat until combined. Heat a lightly greased 6-inch skillet over medium-high heat; remove from heat. Spoon in 2 tablespoons batter; lift and tilt skillet to spread batter. Return to heat; cook 2 to 3 minutes or until brown on 1 side only. (Or cook on a crepemaker according to manufacturer's directions.) Invert skillet over paper towels to remove crepe. Repeat with remaining batter, greasing skillet occasionally.

In the 1970s, crepes were big news, and this rich yet delicate appetizer endures as one of the favorite ways to serve them. Choose the recipe when heading to an upscale potluck, or serve them with a tart green salad as main dish for six.

Upside-Down Marinated Shrimp Bowl

"*I fell in love* with this recipe the first time I made it," says Test Kitchen Director Lynn Blanchard. "It's a very impressive appetizer that's simple to make." Impressive is right! The lemony tomato marinade heightens the shrimp's rich flavor. Because the stacked shrimp maintain the shape of the bowl in which they're marinated, the finished creation makes a stunning centerpiece.

5	pounds fresh large shrimp in shells, peeled and deveined	3	cloves garlic, minced
½	cup olive oil	2	teaspoons grated ginger
½	cup white or red wine vinegar	½	teaspoon salt
1½	teaspoons finely shredded lemon peel	¼	teaspoon ground red pepper
¼	cup lemon juice		Thinly sliced cucumber or cucumber ribbons (optional)
2	tablespoons tomato paste		Thinly sliced red onion (optional)
1	tablespoon honey		

1. In a large kettle bring 5 quarts water and 1 teaspoon salt to boiling. Add the shrimp. Bring to boiling; reduce heat. Simmer, uncovered, for 1 to 3 minutes or until shrimp turn opaque, stirring occasionally. Drain shrimp. Rinse under cold running water; drain again.

2. To arrange shrimp, use a glass bowl that is 7 to 8 inches in diameter and about 4 inches deep. Arrange the shrimp, tails to the center, in a circle to make 1 flat layer. (Only the round backs of shrimp should be visible from the outside of the bowl.) Repeat layers until bowl is filled, pressing down every couple of layers with the bottom of a plate that will fit into the bowl. When bowl is full, press down with plate once again.

3. For marinade, in a screw-top jar combine the olive oil, wine vinegar, lemon peel, lemon juice, tomato paste, honey, garlic, ginger, salt, and ground red pepper. Cover and shake well. Pour marinade over shrimp in bowl. Cover and chill overnight, occasionally placing a flat plate larger than the bowl tightly over the bowl and inverting it to redistribute marinade.

4. Before serving, hold the plate off-center and invert bowl slightly to drain off marinade. Repeat inverting and draining until all marinade is drained. Discard marinade. Place serving platter over bowl; carefully invert bowl to unmold. If desired, arrange cucumber and red onion around shrimp. Makes 20 servings.

Roasted Beet and Goat Cheese Salad

1 pound red baby beets or small beets, rinsed and trimmed
1 tablespoon olive oil
  Salt
  Freshly ground black pepper
⅓ cup olive oil
¼ cup white wine vinegar
2 teaspoons Dijon-style mustard
¼ teaspoon salt
⅛ teaspoon freshly ground black pepper
2 tablespoon finely chopped shallots
10 cups baby salad greens (mesclun) or other mild salad greens
1 8-ounce tube semisoft goat cheese (chèvre or Montrachet), cut into ½-inch rounds

1. If using small beets, halve or quarter. Place beets in a single layer in a shallow baking pan. Drizzle with the 1 tablespoon olive oil; toss to coat. Season with salt and pepper; toss again. Cover with foil and roast in a 425°F oven for 25 minutes. Uncover and roast about 15 minutes more or until fork-tender. Cool; peel the small beets if using. (Baby beets do not need to be peeled.) Cut beets into ½-inch cubes. Place cubes in a medium bowl; set aside.

2. Meanwhile, for dressing, in a screw-top jar combine the ⅓ cup olive oil, the white wine vinegar, Dijon-style mustard, the ¼ teaspoon salt, and the ⅛ teaspoon pepper. Cover and shake well.

3. Add shallots to beets and drizzle with 1 tablespoon of the dressing; toss to coat; set aside. Place the greens in a very large bowl; drizzle with remaining dressing; toss to coat.

4. Divide greens among 8 salad plates. Top with a slice of cheese and some of the beet mixture. Makes 8 servings.

Beets get short shrift in American cuisine—perhaps it's because many cooks here haven't seized upon the secret to bringing out their mellow, sweet flavor: roasting. Add a little goat cheese, a traditional vinaigrette, and you'll unleash a newfound passion for the ruby-red root vegetable.

193

Golden Cheese Wheel

1	package active dry yeast	1/2	cup snipped fresh parsley
2/3	cup warm water (110°F to 115°F)	1/4	teaspoon garlic powder
1 3/4	to 2 cups all-purpose flour	1/8	teaspoon black pepper
2	tablespoons cooking oil	1	slightly beaten egg
1/2	teaspoon sugar	1	tablespoon water
1/2	teaspoon salt	1 1/2	teaspoons sesame seeds
1	beaten egg		
3	cups shredded Muenster cheese (12 ounces)		

If you've "been there, done that" with Brie in puff pastry, try this more rustic and comforting precursor from 1976. A flavorful Muenster cheese filling nestles inside a thin homemade bread crust for a surefire standout on an appetizer spread.

1. In a large mixing bowl dissolve yeast in the warm water. Add 1 cup of the flour, the oil, sugar, and salt. Beat with an electric mixer on low to medium speed for 30 seconds, scraping bowl constantly. Beat on high speed for 3 minutes. Using a wooden spoon, stir in as much of the remaining flour as you can.

2. Turn dough out onto a lightly floured surface. Knead in enough of the remaining all-purpose flour to make a moderately stiff dough that is smooth and elastic (6 to 8 minutes total).

3. Shape dough into a ball. Place in a lightly greased bowl, turning once to grease surface of dough. Cover; let rise in a warm place until double in size (about 1 hour).

4. Punch down dough; turn out onto a lightly floured surface; divide into 2 portions. Cover and let rest 10 minutes. On a lightly floured surface, roll 1 portion into a 13-inch circle. Place circle on a greased 12-inch round pizza pan (dough will extend past edge of pan). Combine the 1 beaten egg, cheese, parsley, garlic powder, and pepper. Spread over dough in pan. Roll remaining dough into 13-inch circle. Place over filling; trim top and bottom doughs to 1/2 inch beyond the edge of the pan; seal and flute edges. Brush top with mixture of 1 slightly beaten egg and the 1 tablespoon water. Sprinkle with sesame seeds. Bake in a 375°F oven for 25 to 30 minutes or until golden brown. Cut in narrow wedges. Serve hot. Makes 12 to 16 servings.

Make-ahead directions: Prepare and shape as directed above. Cover; chill for 1 to 2 hours. Brush with egg-water mixture and sprinkle with sesame seeds. Bake as above.

It's true—soufflés are hardly make-ahead fare. Yet if you're looking to treat guests to a spectacular dish, they're hard to beat. Besides, this one bakes in 65 minutes, which is the perfect amount of time between "would you like a drink?" and "let's eat." So get it ready before your guests arrive, and let the good times roll.

Shallot Soufflé

4 egg yolks	¼ cup butter or margarine
4 egg whites	¼ cup all-purpose flour
1 tablespoon butter or margarine, softened	½ teaspoon salt
	2 dashes bottled hot pepper sauce
2 tablespoons finely shredded Parmesan cheese	1 cup milk
¼ cup finely chopped shallots	1 cup shredded cheddar cheese (4 ounces)

1. Allow egg yolks and egg whites to stand at room temperature for 30 minutes. Spread the 1 tablespoon butter over the bottom and up sides of a 1½-quart soufflé dish. Sprinkle inside of dish with Parmesan cheese, turning dish to coat; set aside.

2. In a medium saucepan cook shallots in the ¼ cup butter until tender but not brown; stir in flour, salt, and hot pepper sauce. Add milk all at once; cook and stir until thickened and bubbly. Remove from heat. Stir in cheddar cheese until melted.

3. In a medium mixing bowl beat egg yolks with an electric mixer on high speed about 5 minutes or until thick and lemon colored. Add cheese mixture, stirring gently to combine; set aside.

4. Thoroughly wash beaters. In a large mixing bowl beat egg whites with an electric mixer on medium to high speed until stiff peaks form (tips stand straight). Fold about 1 cup of the beaten egg whites into the cheese mixture. Fold cheese mixture into remaining egg whites. Spoon soufflé mixture into prepared dish.

5. Bake in a 325°F oven about 65 minutes or until a knife inserted just off center comes out clean. Serve immediately. Makes 6 servings.

Make-ahead directions: Prepare soufflé as above through step 4. Cover and chill for up to 2 hours. Bake as above for 65 to 70 minutes or until a knife inserted just off center comes out clean.

Ever experience the classic French dish Coquilles St. Jacques? While many versions exist, it generally consists of scallops in a luscious wine-laced cream sauce. Here's our sherry-laced take, which makes a stunning dinner-party entrée (as most classic French dishes do). For a special dinner, serve with roasted asparagus and a long grain and wild rice pilaf.

Scallops Elegant

1	pound fresh or frozen sea scallops		1	tablespoon butter
1	tablespoon butter		1	tablespoon all-purpose flour
½	cup finely chopped celery		¼	teaspoon paprika
¼	cup chopped onion		⅛	teaspoon salt
1	small clove garlic, minced		½	cup milk, half-and-half, or light cream
2	tablespoons butter or margarine		2	tablespoons dry sherry
¼	cup fine saltine cracker crumbs		1	ounce Swiss cheese, shredded
1	tablespoon snipped parsley			Hot cooked rice

1. Thaw scallops, if frozen. Rinse scallops; pat dry with paper towels. Cut large scallops in half. Melt 1 tablespoon butter in a large nonstick skillet; add scallops. Cook, gently stirring occasionally, for 2 minutes or just until scallops are opaque. Remove from pan with slotted spoon; set aside.

2. In a medium saucepan cook the celery, onion, and garlic in the 2 tablespoons butter until tender but not brown. Stir in the scallops, cracker crumbs, and parsley. Transfer to a 9-inch pie plate.

3. Melt 1 tablespoon butter in the same saucepan. Stir in flour, paprika, and salt. Add milk all at once. Cook and stir until mixture is thickened and bubbly. Remove from heat; stir in sherry. Pour sauce over scallop mixture; sprinkle with cheese. Bake in a 425°F oven for 15 minutes or until golden. Serve over rice. Makes 4 servings.

Stuffed Chicken in Phyllo

4 skinless, boneless chicken breast halves (about 1¼ pounds total) Salt and black pepper	2 tablespoons butter or margarine
½ of a 4½-ounce round Brie cheese, cut up	1 cup sliced fresh mushrooms, such as oyster, cremini, shiitake, or button
¼ cup chopped hazelnuts (filberts) or pecans, toasted	1 clove garlic, minced
1 tablespoon snipped fresh tarragon or 1 teaspoon dried tarragon, crushed	1 tablespoon all-purpose flour
8 sheets frozen phyllo dough (17×12 inches), thawed	2 teaspoons snipped fresh tarragon or ¼ teaspoon dried tarragon, crushed
⅓ cup butter or margarine, melted	¼ teaspoon salt
	¼ teaspoon black pepper
	¾ cup milk
	2 tablespoons dry white wine or milk

1. Place each breast half between 2 pieces of plastic wrap. Using the flat side of a meat mallet, working from center out, pound each breast half into a rectangle about ⅛ inch thick. Remove wrap.

2. Sprinkle each chicken piece lightly with salt and pepper. Place one-fourth of the cheese 1 inch from bottom edge of each chicken piece; top with one-fourth of the nuts and one-fourth of the 1 tablespoon tarragon. Fold in bottom and sides of each chicken piece; roll up.

3. Unfold phyllo dough. Lay 1 sheet of phyllo dough flat on the work surface; cover remaining sheets with plastic wrap. Brush phyllo with some of the ⅓ cup melted butter. Remove another sheet of dough from stack and place on top of first sheet. Brush with more melted butter. Add 2 more sheets of dough for a total of 4 sheets, brushing each with butter.

4. Cut phyllo stack into two 14×9-inch rectangles. Discard trimmings. Place 1 chicken roll at an end of each rectangle. Roll up, folding in sides. Pinch ends to seal. Using a sharp knife, make 3 diagonal cuts in the top layers of roll. Repeat with remaining phyllo, butter, and chicken rolls. Place wrapped chicken rolls, seam sides down, on a rack in a shallow baking pan. Brush with any remaining melted butter. Bake in a 400°F oven for 15 to 18 minutes or until crisp and golden.

5. Meanwhile, for sauce, in a small saucepan melt the 2 tablespoons butter. Add mushrooms and garlic. Cook and stir until tender. Stir in flour, the 2 teaspoons tarragon, the ¼ teaspoon salt, and the ¼ teaspoon pepper. Add the ¾ cup milk all at once. Cook and stir until thickened and bubbly. Cook and stir 2 minutes more. Stir in white wine or additional milk. Serve sauce with phyllo rolls. Makes 4 servings.

There's just something about multilayered phyllo that never fails to impress—and now that it's widely available, cooking with it is no longer a complicated endeavor! This dish pairs oozy Brie and earthy mushrooms with the airy, light pastry for an elegant exercise in contrast and a stunning dinner-party entrée.

Stuffed with crab, laced with a wine-mushroom sauce, and finished with a sheen of rich Swiss cheese, this perennial pleaser was first developed in 1975 and has been starring in elegant "dinner at eight" parties ever since. Hint: Skip a step—if you can buy pre-pounded chicken breasts from your supermarket meat department, use them!

Crab-Stuffed Chicken

8	skinless, boneless chicken breast halves (about 2½ pounds)	1	6¼-ounce can crabmeat, drained, flaked, and cartilage removed
3	tablespoons butter or margarine	½	cup coarsely crushed saltine crackers (10 crackers)
¼	cup all-purpose flour	2	tablespoons snipped fresh parsley
¾	cup milk	½	teaspoon salt
¾	cup chicken broth		Dash black pepper
⅓	cup dry white wine	2	tablespoons butter or margarine
1	cup chopped fresh mushrooms	1	cup shredded Swiss cheese
¼	cup chopped onion	½	teaspoon paprika
1	tablespoon butter or margarine		

1. Place each chicken breast half between 2 pieces of plastic wrap. Using the flat side of a meat mallet and working from the center out, pound chicken to about ⅛ inch thick. Remove plastic wrap.

2. For sauce, in a medium saucepan melt the 3 tablespoons butter; stir in flour. Add milk, broth, and wine all at once; cook and stir until thickened and bubbly. Set aside.

3. In a medium skillet cook mushrooms and onion in the 1 tablespoon butter until tender but not brown. Stir in crab, cracker crumbs, parsley, salt, and pepper. Stir in 2 tablespoons of the sauce. Top each chicken piece with about ¼ cup of the mushroom mixture. Fold in sides; roll up. Secure with wooden toothpicks, if necessary. In a large skillet brown the chicken rolls, half at a time, in the 2 tablespoons hot butter until brown on all sides.

4. Place chicken rolls, seam sides down, in a 3-quart rectangular baking dish. Pour remaining sauce over all. Bake, covered, in a 350°F oven until chicken is no longer pink (170°F), about 35 minutes. Uncover; sprinkle with Swiss cheese and paprika. Bake about 2 minutes more or until cheese is melted.

5. Transfer chicken to a serving platter. Whisk sauce in baking dish and pass with chicken. Makes 8 servings.

Beef Steaks Wellington

1	17¼-ounce package (2 sheets) frozen puff pastry
8	5-ounce beef tenderloin steaks, cut 1 inch thick
1	tablespoon cooking oil
1	3½-ounce can liver pâté (½ cup)
¼	cup soft bread crumbs
1	tablespoon snipped fresh parsley
½	teaspoon dried basil, crushed
¼	teaspoon garlic salt

	Dash black pepper
1½	cups sliced fresh mushrooms
½	cup sliced green onions
¼	cup butter or margarine
4	teaspoons cornstarch
½	cup dry white wine or beef broth
½	cup water
1½	teaspoons instant beef bouillon granules

1. Thaw pastry according to package directions. Meanwhile, in a large skillet brown steaks, half at a time, in hot oil over medium-high heat for 1 minute on each side. Drain on paper towels; cool. Stir together pâté, bread crumbs, parsley, basil, garlic salt, and pepper. Spread 1 tablespoon of pâté mixture on top of each steak.

2. On lightly floured surface, roll each puff pastry sheet into an 11-inch square; cut each into four 5½-inch squares. Place pastry squares on top of steaks, folding edges under the meat. If necessary, trim pastry so only ½ inch folds under the meat. If desired, cut small shapes from pastry trimmings; moisten and place on top of meat bundles.

3. Place meat bundles, pastry sides up, on a rack in a shallow baking pan. Bake, uncovered, in a 450°F oven for 12 to 15 minutes or until pastry is brown and meat is medium-rare (140°F). If necessary, cover loosely with foil during the last 5 minutes of baking to prevent overbrowning. Let stand 10 minutes before serving. (The temperature of the meat will rise 5° during standing.)

4. Meanwhile, for sauce, in a medium saucepan cook mushrooms and green onions in hot butter until tender. Stir in cornstarch. Add wine, water, and bouillon granules. Cook and stir until thickened and bubbly; cook and stir for 2 minutes more. Serve sauce with meat. Makes 8 servings.

Make-ahead directions: Prepare Beef Steaks Wellington as above through step 2. Cover and freeze on baking sheet for about 1 hour or until firm. Transfer to freezer bags or containers and freeze up to 3 months. To serve, place frozen bundles, pastry sides up, on a rack in a shallow baking pan. Bake in a 450°F oven for 30 to 35 minutes or until pastry is brown and meat is medium-rare. If necessary, cover loosely with foil during the last 10 minutes to prevent overbrowning. Let stand 10 minutes before serving.

Beef Wellington—rich beef tenderloin spread with liver pâté and wrapped in a buttery crust—has long been a favorite for spectacular entertaining. We recently updated this classic dinner-party dish with make-ahead directions so all this elegance can be wrapped up, ready, and waiting in your freezer for just the right occasion.

Grilled Beef Tenderloin with Mediterranean Relish

2	teaspoons dried oregano, crushed
2	teaspoons cracked black pepper
1½	teaspoons finely shredded lemon peel
3	cloves garlic, minced
1	3- to 4-pound center-cut beef tenderloin
2	Japanese eggplants, halved lengthwise
2	red or yellow sweet peppers, halved lengthwise and seeded
1	sweet onion (such as Walla Walla or Vidalia), cut into ½-inch slices
2	tablespoons olive oil
2	plum tomatoes, chopped
2	tablespoons chopped, pitted kalamata olives
2	tablespoons snipped fresh basil
1	tablespoon balsamic vinegar
¼	to ½ teaspoon salt
⅛	teaspoon ground black pepper

1. In a small bowl combine oregano, cracked pepper, lemon peel, and 2 cloves of the garlic. Use your fingers to rub the mixture onto all sides of the meat.

2. In a grill with a cover, arrange hot coals around a drip pan. Test for medium-hot heat above the pan. Place meat on grill rack over drip pan. Brush eggplants, sweet peppers, and onion slices with olive oil. Arrange vegetables on edges of grill rack directly over coals. Cover and grill for 10 to 12 minutes or until vegetables are tender, turning once. Remove vegetables from grill; set aside. Cover grill and continue grilling meat for 25 to 30 minutes more or until a meat thermometer inserted in the center registers 135°F for medium-rare doneness. Cover; let stand for 15 minutes before slicing. Temperature of meat will rise to 145°F upon standing.

3. Meanwhile, for relish, coarsely chop grilled vegetables. In a medium bowl combine grilled vegetables, tomatoes, olives, basil, the remaining garlic clove, the vinegar, salt, and the ground black pepper. Serve the beef with relish. Makes 10 servings.

Showstoppers

Smoke cooking and dry rubs are culinary hot buttons today, but guess what? This succulent recipe dates back to 1977, proving that we've long been fans of great smoke cooking. How good is this recipe? Sharon Stilwell, who reigned as Test Kitchen director from 1978 to 1999, named this as a tip-top favorite, as did Nancy Byal, who was the executive food editor of *Better Homes and Gardens* magazine for many years.

Chinese Smoked Ribs

2 tablespoons granulated sugar	1/4 cup catsup
1/2 teaspoon salt	1/4 cup soy sauce
1/4 teaspoon paprika	2 tablespoons packed brown sugar
1/4 teaspoon ground turmeric	2 tablespoons water
1/4 teaspoon celery seeds	1 teaspoon grated fresh ginger or
1/4 teaspoon dry mustard	1 teaspoon ground ginger
4 pounds pork loin back ribs or meaty spareribs	4 cups alder or oak wood chips

1. For rub, in a small bowl combine granulated sugar, salt, paprika, turmeric, celery seeds, and dry mustard. Trim fat from ribs. Place ribs in a shallow dish. Sprinkle the rub evenly over ribs; rub in with your fingers. Cover and marinate in the refrigerator for 6 to 24 hours.

2. For sauce, in a small bowl combine catsup, soy sauce, brown sugar, water, and ginger. Cover and refrigerate for 6 to 24 hours.

3. At least 1 hour before smoke cooking, soak wood chips in enough water to cover. Drain off water before using.

4. In a charcoal grill, arrange medium-hot coals around a drip pan. Test for medium heat above the pan. Sprinkle half of the drained wood chips over the coals. Place ribs, bone side down, on the grill rack over drip pan. (Or place ribs in a rib rack; place on grill rack.) Cover and smoke for 1¼ to 1½ hours or until ribs are tender, brushing once with sauce during the last 15 minutes of cooking. Add more coals and wood chips as needed. (In a gas grill, preheat grill. Reduce heat to medium. Adjust for indirect cooking. Add drained wood chips according to the grill manufacturer's directions. Smoke as above, except place ribs in a roasting pan.) Before serving, brush ribs with the remaining sauce. Makes 6 servings.

Boursin Mashed Potatoes

3½ pounds potatoes, peeled and cut into
2-inch chunks (about 10 medium
potatoes)
2 5.2-ounce packages boursin cheese
with garlic and herbs

½ cup whole milk, half-and-half, or light
cream
Salt and black pepper

1. In a large saucepan or Dutch oven cover potatoes with boiling water. Cook, covered, for 20 to 25 minutes or until tender. Drain; return potatoes to saucepan or Dutch oven. Mash with potato masher or beat with mixer on low speed until smooth. Add cheese; beat until combined. Beat in milk until combined. Season with salt and pepper.

2. Spoon potato mixture into a 2-quart casserole. Cover and bake in a 350°F oven for 25 minutes or until heated through. Makes 8 to 10 servings.

Make-ahead directions: Prepare Boursin Mashed Potatoes as above through step 1. Spoon into a microwave-safe 2-quart casserole. Cover; refrigerate up to 24 hours. To serve, uncover potatoes. Cover with vented plastic wrap. Microwave on 100 percent power (high) for 15 to 18 minutes or until heated through, stirring once. (Or bake, covered, in a 350°F oven about 1½ hours or until heated through.)

Everything about this side dish makes it a favorite. First, you can put away your measuring spoons—the boursin cheese is flavored with plenty of garlic and herbs to go around. Second, it can be made ahead. And third, it's simply a rich and wonderful dish.

French Chocolate Coffee Cake

4 to 4½ cups all-purpose flour	**2** tablespoons sugar
2 packages active dry yeast	**½** teaspoon ground cinnamon
¾ cup sugar	**¼** cup all-purpose flour
⅔ cup water	**¼** cup sugar
½ cup butter, cut up	**1** teaspoon ground cinnamon
1 5-ounce can evaporated milk (⅔ cup)	**¼** cup butter
½ teaspoon salt	**¼** cup chopped walnuts or pecans
4 egg yolks	
1 cup semisweet chocolate pieces (6 ounces)	

1. In a large mixing bowl stir together 1½ cups of the flour and the yeast; set aside. In a medium saucepan heat and stir the ¾ cup sugar, the water, the ½ cup butter, ⅓ cup of the evaporated milk, and the salt just until warm (120°F to 130°F) and butter almost melts. Add milk mixture to flour mixture; add egg yolks. Beat with an electric mixer on low to medium speed 30 seconds, scraping the sides of bowl constantly. Beat on high speed 3 minutes. Using a wooden spoon, stir in as much remaining flour as you can.

2. Turn dough out onto a lightly floured surface. Knead in enough of the remaining flour to make a moderately soft dough that is smooth and elastic (3 to 5 minutes total). Shape dough into a ball. Place in a lightly greased bowl, turning once to grease surface. Cover and let rise in a warm place until doubled (about 2 hours). Punch dough down. Turn dough out onto a lightly floured surface. Cover; let rest for 10 minutes.

3. Meanwhile, in a small saucepan combine the remaining evaporated milk, ¾ cup of the chocolate pieces, the 2 tablespoons sugar, and the ½ teaspoon cinnamon. Cook and stir over low heat until chocolate is melted. Remove from heat; cool.

4. Grease a 10-inch tube pan; set aside. Roll dough into an 18×10-inch rectangle. Spread chocolate mixture to within 1 inch of the edges. Starting from a long side, roll up dough. Pinch seam to seal. Place, seam side up, in prepared pan. Pinch ends together.

5. In a small bowl combine the ¼ cup flour, the ¼ cup sugar, and the 1 teaspoon cinnamon. Using a pastry blender, cut in the ¼ cup butter until mixture resembles coarse crumbs. Stir in remaining chocolate pieces and nuts. Sprinkle over dough in pan. Cover; let rise in a warm place until nearly double (about 1 hour). Bake in a 350°F oven about 50 minutes or until bread sounds hollow when lightly tapped. Cool in pan on a wire rack for 15 minutes. Remove from pan; cool for 45 minutes. Serve warm. Makes 12 to 16 servings.

This luscious coffee cake was the inspiration behind this book. Thirty-year Test Kitchen veteran Maryellyn Krantz made it for a young Test Kitchen colleague, Jennifer Kalinowski, to celebrate Jennifer's trip to France. When Maryellyn learned that Jennifer wasn't familiar with this sumptuous recipe, that got everyone thinking about all the other wonderful recipes in the files that were in danger of being forgotten. The rest is … in this book!

Christmas Kringle

¾	cup butter, softened	3	cups all-purpose flour
1	package active dry yeast	1	egg
¼	cup warm water (105°F to 115°F)	1	tablespoon water
¾	cup milk		**Sweet Filling**
1	egg, slightly beaten	¼	cup finely chopped blanched almonds
¼	cup sugar	1	tablespoon sugar
1	teaspoon salt		

1. Roll butter between sheets of waxed paper into a 10×6-inch rectangle. Chill for 15 minutes. Meanwhile, in a large mixing bowl dissolve yeast in the warm water; let stand 5 minutes. In small saucepan heat milk just until warm (105°F to 115°F); add to yeast with beaten egg, the ¼ cup sugar, and salt. Stir in flour until moistened. Dough will be soft.

2. Turn out dough onto a surface sprinkled with 2 tablespoons flour; to make rolling easier, turn dough to coat lightly with flour. Roll into a 12-inch square. Remove top sheet of waxed paper from chilled butter rectangle and invert onto half of the dough square. Remove remaining waxed paper sheet. Fold over the opposite dough half to cover butter, and form a 12×6-inch rectangle; pinch to seal seam and ends. Cover; let rest 10 minutes. Roll out again into a 12-inch square; fold into thirds. Place on a baking sheet or tray. Cover with plastic wrap and chill 30 minutes. Repeat rolling, folding, and chilling twice more. (If desired, wrap, leaving room for dough to expand, and chill up to 24 hours.)

3. Cut dough lengthwise into 3 strips. Roll one strip into an 18×4-inch rectangle. Combine egg and the 1 tablespoon water; brush some on rectangle. Sprinkle one-third of the Sweet Filling along the center of the strip. Bring sides together to enclose filling and form an 18-inch roll; pinch edges to seal. Place roll, seam side down, onto a parchment paper-lined 15×10×1-inch baking pan, bringing ends together to shape roll into an oval. Press ends together to seal; flatten oval to ½-inch thickness.

4. Brush surface with egg-water mixture and sprinkle with 4 teaspoons of the chopped almonds and 1 teaspoon of the sugar. Repeat with remaining dough and filling to make 2 more ovals. Cover and let rest for 30 minutes. Bake in a 375°F oven for 20 to 25 minutes or until golden. Remove from baking sheets; cool. Makes 24 servings.

Sweet Filling: In a small mixing bowl beat ¼ cup butter, softened, with an electric mixer on medium to high speed for 30 seconds. Add ¾ cup sugar and beat until combined. Stir in 2 cups dried tart cherries and/or coarsely chopped pecans.

Chocolate Crème Brûlée

2	cups whipping cream	1	teaspoon vanilla
3	ounces semisweet or bittersweet	¼	teaspoon salt
	chocolate, chopped	2	tablespoons sugar
5	slightly beaten egg yolks		Whipped cream
¼	cup sugar		Strawberries or raspberries

1. In a medium heavy saucepan heat and stir ⅓ cup of the whipping cream and the chocolate over low heat until chocolate is melted. Remove from heat. Using a whisk, gradually add the remaining cream.

2. In a large bowl whisk together the egg yolks, the ¼ cup sugar, vanilla, and salt. Gradually whisk the cream mixture into the egg yolk mixture.

3. Place six ¾-cup ramekins or 6-ounce custard cups in a baking pan. Set pan on the oven rack. Pour the egg mixture into the ramekins or custard cups. Pour enough boiling water or very hot water into the baking pan around the ramekins or custard cups to cover the bottom half of the dishes. Bake in a 325°F oven for 35 to 40 minutes or until a knife inserted near center comes out clean. Transfer dishes from pan with water to a wire rack.

4. Immediately after removing dishes from oven, place 2 tablespoons sugar in a small heavy skillet or saucepan. Cook over medium-high heat until sugar just begins to melt, shaking skillet occasionally to heat sugar evenly. (Do not stir.) Reduce heat to low. Cook until sugar is melted and golden (watch closely, as sugar melts quickly). Using a wooden spoon, stir as necessary after sugar begins to melt and mixture bubbles. Drizzle melted sugar in a zigzag pattern over brûlée in ramekins. Cool about 1 hour before serving. Or cool slightly, cover, and chill in the refrigerator for up to 6 hours. If chilled, let stand at room temperature 30 minutes before serving. Serve with whipped cream and berries. Makes 6 servings.

For this opulent version of the French classic, we added chocolate and simplifed the caramelized sugar process too—now it's done on top of the stove instead of under the broiler. The result—an ever-so-thin glaze of melted sugar on top of a smooth, rich custard—is as "ooh-la-la" as ever.

Mango Buttercream Cake

1 24-ounce jar mango slices in light syrup	**2** 9- or 10-inch layers white cake, cooled
1 cup sugar	**36** to 50 cream-filled cylinder cookies (depending on size of cake)
6 beaten eggs yolks	Mango slices (optional)
3 tablespoons orange liqueur or apricot brandy	Chopped pistachio nuts (optional)
2 cups (1 pound) unsalted butter, softened	

1. For mango buttercream, drain the mango slices, reserving a few slices for garnish. Place in a food processor bowl or blender container. Cover and process or blend until smooth. (You should have 1½ cups puree.) In a heavy medium saucepan gently simmer mango puree over medium-low heat until it is reduced to 1 cup, about 25 minutes, stirring frequently to prevent scorching.

2. Stir the sugar into mango puree in saucepan. Cook and stir over medium heat until bubbly. Remove from heat. Gradually stir about 1 cup of the hot mixture into the beaten egg yolks. Return the egg yolk mixture to the saucepan. Bring to a gentle boil; reduce heat. Cook and stir for 2 minutes more. Remove from heat.

3. Quickly cool the mixture by placing the saucepan into a bowl of ice water. Stir in the liqueur. Stir for 2 minutes. Transfer mixture to a medium bowl. Cover; chill for 1 hour.

4. In a large mixing bowl beat the butter with an electric mixer on medium speed until fluffy. Pour cooled mango mixture into beaten butter. Beat until fluffy. Reserve 1½ cups of the buttercream for garnish.

5. Using a long, serrated knife, split each cake layer in half horizontally. Place 1 cake layer on a plate. Frost with about ⅓ cup of the buttercream. Repeat with 2 more cake layers and ⅔ cup more of the buttercream. Top with the last cake layer. Spread remaining buttercream on top and sides of cake layers.

6. Lightly press cookies into buttercream, around sides of cake, cookie ends even with the bottom of cake and cookie tops extending beyond height of cake. Tie cookies with a long fancy ribbon to secure, if desired.

7. Spoon reserved 1½ cups buttercream into a pastry bag fitted with a large star tip. Pipe buttercream into small mounds on top of cake. Chill cake or serve immediately. Before serving, arrange mango slices in center of cake and sprinkle nuts over cake, if desired. Makes 12 servings.

Caramel Apple Crepes

¾ cup all-purpose flour	4 teaspoons walnut oil or cooking oil
⅓ cup water	Caramel Apple Sauce
⅓ cup milk	Candied Nuts
2 eggs	Vanilla ice cream (optional)
2 tablespoons sugar	

1. For crepes, in a blender container combine the flour, water, milk, eggs, sugar, and oil. Cover and blend until smooth, stopping and scraping the sides as necessary.

2. Heat a lightly greased 6-inch skillet over medium heat; remove from heat. Spoon 2 tablespoons of batter into skillet; lift and tilt skillet to spread batter evenly. Return skillet to heat; brown on 1 side only. Invert skillet over paper towels to remove crepe from pan. Repeat with remaining batter, making 12 crepes total.

3. Prepare Caramel Apple Sauce and Candied Nuts.

4. Fold the crepes in half, browned sides out. Fold in half again, forming triangles. Place 2 crepes each on 6 dessert plates.

5. To serve, pour warm Caramel Apple Sauce over crepes. Sprinkle with some of the Candied Nuts. If desired, serve with vanilla ice cream. Makes 6 servings.

Caramel Apple Sauce: In a large saucepan stir together 1 cup packed brown sugar and 4 teaspoons cornstarch. Stir in 1 cup whipping cream; 2 tablespoons apple brandy, brandy, or apple juice; and 1 tablespoon butter or margarine. Add 2 cups thinly sliced apples. Cook and stir over medium heat until thickened and bubbly. Cook and stir for 2 minutes more.

Candied Nuts: Line a baking sheet with foil; butter the foil. Set aside. In a large heavy skillet combine 1½ cups pecan halves, ½ cup sugar, 2 tablespoons butter, and ½ teaspoon vanilla. Cook over medium-high heat, shaking skillet occasionally, until sugar begins to melt. Do not stir. Reduce heat to low. Continue cooking until sugar is golden brown, stirring occasionally. Remove skillet from heat. Pour nut mixture onto prepared baking sheet. Cool completely. Break into clusters. Store tightly covered in the refrigerator up to 3 weeks.

Zuppa Inglese

4 eggs	¼ cup butter
Cream Filling	¼ cup rum
2 cups all-purpose flour	¼ cup cherry, apricot, or apple brandy
2 teaspoons baking powder	1½ cups whipping cream
2 cups sugar	¼ cup chopped candied fruits and peels
1 cup milk	2 tablespoons sliced almonds, toasted

1. Allow eggs to stand at room temperature for 30 minutes. Meanwhile, prepare Cream Filling; cover, and chill. Lightly grease bottoms of two 9×1½-inch round cake pans. Line bottoms of pans with waxed paper. Grease and lightly flour paper and sides of pans; set aside. In a small bowl stir together the flour and baking powder; set aside.

2. In a large mixing bowl beat the eggs with an electric mixer on high speed about 4 minutes or until thick. Gradually add sugar, beating on medium speed for 4 to 5 minutes or until light and fluffy. Add the flour mixture; beat on low to medium speed just until combined. In a small saucepan heat and stir the milk and butter until butter melts; add to batter, beating until combined.

3. Spread batter into prepared pans. Bake in a 350°F oven for 30 minutes or until a toothpick inserted near the center comes out clean. Cool in pans on a wire rack for 10 minutes. Remove from pans; cool completely.

4. To assemble, split each cake layer in half horizontally. Place one layer, cut side up, on serving plate. Mix rum and brandy; carefully brush 2 tablespoons of the mixture over the cake layer on plate. Spread with one-third of the Cream Filling (about ⅔ cup). Repeat layers twice more. Top with the final cake layer, cut side down. Brush the remaining 2 tablespoons rum mixture over the top. Cover and chill cake for 4 to 6 hours.

5. Just before serving, whip cream to stiff peaks. Frost top and sides of cake with whipped cream. Garnish with candied fruits and peels and almonds. Makes 12 servings.

Cream Filling: In a heavy medium saucepan stir together ½ cup sugar, 4 teaspoons cornstarch, and ¼ teaspoon salt. Stir in 2 cups half-and-half or light cream. If desired, add 1 vanilla bean, split lengthwise. Cook and stir over medium heat until thickened and bubbly. Cook and stir 1 minute more. Gradually stir half of the hot mixture into 4 beaten egg yolks. Return all of the egg yolk mixture to saucepan. Bring to a gentle boil; reduce heat. Cook and stir for 2 minutes. Remove from heat. Remove vanilla bean. Pour into a medium bowl. If not using vanilla bean, stir in 1 teaspoon liquid vanilla. Place bowl of pastry cream in a bowl of ice water; chill for 5 minutes, stirring occasionally. Cover surface with plastic wrap. Chill in the refrigerator until serving time; do not stir.

Zuppa Inglese literally translates as "English soup," and some believe that the name comes from the dessert's resemblance to the trifle, a classic British dessert. With liquor-infused sponge layers, cream filling, and whipped cream, we see the similarities, but this is more a layer cake than a layered dessert. Try it soon, and you'll see why we think it deserves a prominent place next to the other great Italian desserts, such as tiramisu.

This is the sort of exquisite treat you expect to find in a European pastry shop (which, incidentally, is where Nancy Byal, former executive food editor of *Better Homes and Gardens* magazine, discovered it in the 1970s). The name (pronounced bowm-KYOO-kin) roughly translates as "tree cake," because when sliced, the layers resemble rings on a crosscut tree.

Baumkuchen

10 egg whites	½ cup cornstarch
10 egg yolks	¼ teaspoon salt
¾ cup butter, softened	¼ cup sugar
¾ cup sugar	Chocolate Glaze
2 teaspoons finely shredded lemon peel	Vanilla Glaze
1 teaspoon vanilla	Fresh mint sprigs (optional)
1 cup all-purpose flour	Fresh raspberries (optional)

1. Allow egg whites and yolks to stand at room temperature for 30 minutes. Meanwhile, grease an 8-inch springform pan; set aside.

2. In a medium mixing bowl beat egg yolks with an electric mixer on high speed for 5 minutes or until thick and lemon colored; set aside. In an extra large mixing bowl beat butter with an electric mixer on medium to high speed for 30 seconds. Gradually add the ¾ cup sugar, lemon peel, and vanilla. Add egg yolks, beating well. In a small bowl stir together the flour, cornstarch, and salt; stir flour mixture into butter mixture.

3. Thoroughly wash beaters. In the large mixing bowl beat egg whites on medium speed until soft peaks form (tips curl). Gradually add the ¼ cup sugar, beating on high speed until stiff peaks form (tips stand straight). Fold egg white mixture into egg yolk mixture.

4. Evenly spread ⅓ cup of batter in bottom of prepared pan. Place under broiler 5 inches from heat; broil for 1 to 2 minutes or until lightly browned. (Give pan a half-turn for even browning, if needed.) Do not overbrown. Remove from broiler. Spread another ⅓ cup batter on top of first layer. Broil as before, turning if necessary. Repeat, making about 17 layers. Cool 10 minutes. Loosen cake and remove sides of pan; cool completely.

5. Cut into 12 wedges. Place wedges on wire rack with waxed paper beneath. Spread Vanilla Glaze over 6 wedges; spread Chocolate Glaze over remainder, covering tops and letting some glaze drip down the sides. Drizzle vanilla-glazed wedges with chocolate glaze and drizzle chocolate-glazed wedges with vanilla glaze. Let dry. Garnish with mint sprigs and fresh raspberries, if desired. Makes 12 servings.

Chocolate Glaze: Melt 1½ ounces unsweetened chocolate and 2 tablespoons butter over low heat, stirring constantly; remove from heat. Stir in 1½ cups sifted powdered sugar and 1 teaspoon vanilla. Add 2 to 3 tablespoons of boiling water to make a thin glaze.

Vanilla Glaze: Combine 2 cups sifted powdered sugar and 1 teaspoon vanilla. Add enough milk (2 to 3 tablespoons) to make a thin glaze.

Burnt Sugar-Candy Bar Cake

Here's a relative newcomer to our favorites file; it appeared in January 2000. We enjoy the rich flavor the caramelized sugar gives to the cake, and so do our readers who request the recipe often. Another reason to like it? You can personalize the cake by topping it with any candy bars you love most.

¾ cup granulated sugar
¾ cup hot water
3 cups all-purpose flour
1½ teaspoons baking powder
¼ teaspoon baking soda
1½ cups granulated sugar
⅔ cup butter, softened
2 egg yolks

2 teaspoons vanilla
2 egg whites
Browned Butter Frosting
1½ cups finely chopped assorted candy
    bars
Coarsely chopped assorted candy bars
    (optional)*

1. Grease and lightly flour three 8×1½-inch round baking pans or two 9×2-inch round baking pans. In a large skillet cook the ¾ cup granulated sugar over medium-high heat until the sugar just begins to melt (do not stir). Reduce heat; cook until sugar is golden brown, about 1 to 3 minutes more, stirring constantly.

2. Carefully stir in hot water (syrup will form lumps). Bring mixture to boiling; reduce heat. Continue stirring until mixture is free of lumps. Remove from heat. Pour syrup into a large glass measuring cup. Add additional water to equal 1¾ cups liquid. Set aside to cool.

3. In a large bowl stir together flour, baking powder, and baking soda. In another large mixing bowl beat together the 1½ cups granulated sugar, the ⅔ cup butter, egg yolks, and vanilla with an electric mixer on medium speed about 1 minute or until mixture is smooth. Alternately add flour mixture and sugar syrup to egg yolk mixture, beating on low speed after each addition just until combined.

4. Wash and dry beaters thoroughly. In a medium mixing bowl beat egg whites until stiff peaks form (tips stand straight). Gently fold whites into batter.

5. Divide batter into prepared pans; spread evenly. Bake in a 350°F oven for 25 to 30 minutes or until wooden toothpicks inserted near centers comes out clean. Cool in pans on wire racks for 10 minutes. Remove cakes from pans. Transfer cakes to wire racks; cool completely. Prepare Browned Butter Frosting.

6. To assemble, spread ½ cup Browned Butter Frosting over bottoms of 2 of the cake layers. Sprinkle each frosted layer with half of the finely chopped candy bars. Stack these layers on a cake plate, frosted sides up. Place the third (unfrosted) layer on top, rounded side up.

7. Spread remaining frosting on top and sides of cake. If desired, garnish with the coarsely chopped candy bar pieces. Makes 16 servings.

Browned Butter Frosting: In a small saucepan heat and stir ½ cup butter (no substitutes) over low heat until melted. Continue heating until butter turns a nut-brown color. Remove from heat; cool for 5 minutes. In a large mixing bowl beat together two 3-ounce packages of softened cream cheese with 3 tablespoons butter until combined. Beat in about 2 cups sifted powdered sugar. Beat in the browned butter and 1 teaspoon vanilla. Gradually beat in an additional 4½ cups sifted powdered sugar and 2 to 3 teaspoons milk until the frosting is of spreading consistency.

In *1971,* some clever cook got the idea of imbuing a cheesecake with pumpkin-pie flavors. The result took honors in the Prize Tested Recipe contest, and it's been a holiday favorite ever since. It's also a favorite of retired Test Kitchen director Sharon Stilwell.

Pumpkin Cheesecake

1½ cups zwieback crumbs (about 17 crackers) or 1½ cups graham cracker crumbs (about 20 squares)	3 tablespoons all-purpose flour
⅓ cup sugar	1½ teaspoons vanilla
3 tablespoons butter, melted	1 teaspoon ground cinnamon
2 8-ounce packages cream cheese, softened	½ teaspoon ground ginger
1 cup half-and-half or light cream	½ teaspoon ground nutmeg
1 cup canned pumpkin	¼ teaspoon salt
¾ cup sugar	4 eggs
	1 8-ounce carton dairy sour cream
	2 tablespoons sugar
	½ teaspoon vanilla

1. For crust, combine crumbs, the ⅓ cup sugar, and melted butter. Press onto bottom and about 2 inches up sides of an ungreased 9-inch springform pan. Bake in a 325°F oven for 5 minutes; set aside.

2. For filling, in a large mixing bowl beat cream cheese, half-and-half, pumpkin, the ¾ cup sugar, flour, the 1½ teaspoons vanilla, cinnamon, ginger, nutmeg, and salt with an electric mixer until smooth. Add eggs, beating on low speed just until combined.

3. Spoon filling into crust-lined pan. Place springform pan in a shallow baking pan. Bake in a 325°F oven for 1 hour or until center appears nearly set when gently shaken.

4. Combine the sour cream, the 2 tablespoons sugar, and the ½ teaspoon vanilla; spread over cheesecake. Bake 5 minutes more.

5. Cool in springform pan on a wire rack for 15 minutes. Loosen crust from sides of pan with a thin-bladed knife or narrow spatula and cool 30 minutes more. Remove sides of pan; cool 1 hour. Cover and chill at least 4 hours or up to 24 hours. Makes 16 servings.

To store cheesecake: Cover tightly with plastic wrap. Chill in refrigerator for up to 3 days. Or seal a whole cheesecake or individual pieces in a freezer bag, in an airtight container, or wrapped in heavy foil. Freeze a whole cheesecake for up to a month and pieces for up to 2 weeks. To serve, loosen the covering slightly. Thaw a whole cheesecake in the refrigerator for 24 hours. Thaw individual pieces at room temperature about 30 minutes.

220

Metric Information

The charts on this page provide a guide for converting measurements from the U.S. customary system, which is used throughout this book, to the metric system.

Product Differences

Most of the ingredients called for in the recipes in this book are available in most countries. However, some are known by different names. Here are some common American ingredients and their possible counterparts:

■ Sugar (white) is granulated, fine granulated, or castor sugar.

■ Powdered sugar is icing sugar.

■ All-purpose flour is enriched, bleached or unbleached white household flour. When self-rising flour is used in place of all-purpose flour in a recipe that calls for leavening, omit the leavening agent (baking soda or baking powder) and salt.

■ Light-colored corn syrup is golden syrup.

■ Cornstarch is cornflour.

■ Baking soda is bicarbonate of soda.

■ Vanilla or vanilla extract is vanilla essence.

■ Green, red, or yellow sweet peppers are capsicums or bell peppers.

■ Golden raisins are sultanas.

Volume and Weight

The United States traditionally uses cup measures for liquid and solid ingredients. The chart below shows the approximate imperial and metric equivalents. If you are accustomed to weighing solid ingredients, the following approximate equivalents will be helpful.

■ 1 cup butter, castor sugar, or rice = 8 ounces = ½ pound = 250 grams

■ 1 cup flour = 4 ounces = ¼ pound = 125 grams

■ 1 cup icing sugar = 5 ounces = 150 grams

Canadian and U.S. volume for a cup measure is 8 fluid ounces (237 ml), but the standard metric equivalent is 250 ml.

1 British imperial cup is 10 fluid ounces.

In Australia, 1 tablespoon equals 20 ml, and there are 4 teaspoons in the Australian tablespoon.

Spoon measures are used for smaller amounts of ingredients. Although the size of the tablespoon varies slightly in different countries, for practical purposes and for recipes in this book, a straight substitution is all that's necessary. Measurements made using cups or spoons always should be level unless stated otherwise.

Common Weight Range Replacements

Imperial / U.S.	Metric
½ ounce	15 g
1 ounce	25 g or 30 g
4 ounces (¼ pound)	115 g or 125 g
8 ounces (½ pound)	225 g or 250 g
16 ounces (1 pound)	450 g or 500 g
1¼ pounds	625 g
1½ pounds	750 g
2 pounds or 2¼ pounds	1,000 g or 1 Kg

Oven Temperature Equivalents

Fahrenheit Setting	Celsius Setting*	Gas Setting
300°F	150°C	Gas Mark 2 (very low)
325°F	160°C	Gas Mark 3 (low)
350°F	180°C	Gas Mark 4 (moderate)
375°F	190°C	Gas Mark 5 (moderate)
400°F	200°C	Gas Mark 6 (hot)
425°F	220°C	Gas Mark 7 (hot)
450°F	230°C	Gas Mark 8 (very hot)
475°F	240°C	Gas Mark 9 (very hot)
500°F	260°C	Gas Mark 10 (extremely hot)
Broil	Broil	Grill

*Electric and gas ovens may be calibrated using celsius. However, for an electric oven, increase celsius setting 10 to 20 degrees when cooking above 160°C. For convection or forced air ovens (gas or electric) lower the temperature setting 25°F/10°C when cooking at all heat levels.

Baking Pan Sizes

Imperial / U.S.	Metric
9×1½-inch round cake pan	22- or 23×4-cm (1.5 L)
9×1½-inch pie plate	22- or 23×4-cm (1 L)
8×8×2-inch square cake pan	20×5-cm (2 L)
9×9×2-inch square cake pan	22- or 23×4.5-cm (2.5 L)
11×7×1½-inch baking pan	28×17×4-cm (2 L)
2-quart rectangular baking pan	30×19×4.5-cm (3 L)
13×9×2-inch baking pan	34×22×4.5-cm (3.5 L)
15×10×1-inch jelly roll pan	40×25×2-cm
9×5×3-inch loaf pan	23×13×8-cm (2 L)
2-quart casserole	2 L

U.S. / Standard Metric Equivalents

⅛ teaspoon	= 0.5 ml
¼ teaspoon	= 1 ml
½ teaspoon	= 2 ml
1 teaspoon	= 5 ml
1 tablespoon	= 15 ml
2 tablespoons	= 25 ml
¼ cup = 2 fluid ounces	= 50 ml
⅓ cup = 3 fluid ounces	= 75 ml
½ cup = 4 fluid ounces	= 125 ml
⅔ cup = 5 fluid ounces	= 150 ml
¾ cup = 6 fluid ounces	= 175 ml
1 cup = 8 fluid ounces	= 250 ml
2 cups = 1 pint	= 500 ml
1 quart	= 1 litre